THE SPIRITUAL AWAKENING PROCESS

Aletheia Luna & Mateo Sol

Copyright

The Spiritual Awakening Process
Copyright © Aletheia Luna and Mateo Sol, 2019
ISBN: 9781370002900

All rights reserved. No part of this book may be reproduced or transmitted in any form or by any means, electronic or mechanical, including photocopying, recording, or by any information storage and retrieval system, without permission in writing by the authors.

The information contained in this book is intended to be educational and not for diagnosis, prescription, or treatment of any health disorder whatsoever. This information should not replace consultation with a competent healthcare professional. The authors are in no way liable for any misuse of the material.

"What is this precious love and laughter

Budding in our hearts?

It is the glorious sound

Of a soul waking up!"

— **Hafiz**

To those who are lost, confused, and alone.
To those who crave more depth.
To those waking up:
This is for you.

Table of Contents

Introduction 1

Chapter 1: Crisis and the Spiritual Calling 9

Chapter 2: Spiritual Awakening Stages 19

Chapter 3: Spiritual Awakening Symptoms 25

Chapter 4: The Three Worlds of the
    Spiritual Journey 37

Chapter 5: The Spiritual Emergency 48

Chapter 6: Are You Experiencing Soul Loss? 80

Chapter 7: How to Practice Soul Retrieval 90

Chapter 8: Inner Child Work 100

Chapter 9: Self-Love 121

Chapter 10: Shadow Work 141

Chapter 11: Spiritual Bypassing Traps 165

Chapter 12: Soul Communication 186

Conclusion 207

Closing Prayer 212

References 214

Bibliography 219

About the Authors 221

Other Books by the Authors 222

Introduction

Humanity has reached a critical crossroads in its evolution. We have made huge, unprecedented strides economically, technologically, and scientifically. As a result, many of us are experiencing enormous material benefits and freedoms more than ever before. But there is a dark side. These advancements have also given birth to a range of disturbing problems that have resulted in large-scale Soul Loss.

When we are cut off from the Soul, we are cut off from ourselves, each other, and the world. It is then that we see people becoming increasingly anxious, depressed, and isolated from each other. It is then that we see humanity at large lacking the meaning and purpose of being connected to something beyond the material self.

The consequence of falling into a state of cold rationalism and mechanistic reductionism is that, as a species, we see the world and each other as objects to be used and discarded. Being severed from the Soul, the human being becomes deranged. Illnesses of every kind begin to emerge, starting within the body as chronic sicknesses and cating disorders – ending with mental illnesses, existential crises, paranoia, hatred, suicide, murder, and the psychotic abuse of our most innocent members of society.

Most of us can sense that behind the facade of normality, something is terribly wrong. The world's population is increasing rapidly, our ecological systems are suffering tremendously, resources are becoming scarce, food is being polluted and genetically modified, the rich continue to get richer, and the poor, poorer, and our financial systems are as unstable as ever.

Intuitively, many of us know that something in our lives and the world around us desperately needs to change. We're beginning to realize that we need to radically adjust our way of thinking, perceiving, being, and behaving. We're waking up to the need to shift our focus from the external world to the boundlessly internal one.

In other words, we need to learn how to reconnect with our Souls.

Our world is so caught up in progressing externally; in the evolution of our economies, in the advancement of our technologies, and as always, in the improvement of our material lives. But we have forgotten to explore our internal lives. And our neglect shows itself in the constant chaos and suffering we create for ourselves and the surrounding world. As a result of this profound inner emptiness and turmoil, the purpose of this book is to offer a path that can help heal these wounds. We call this process *Inner Work*. Inner Work is a practice that involves going inwards and working with our Souls so that we may heal our deeply buried grief, anger, and fear.

We are all craving for Wholeness; for something that takes us beyond the mundane and ordinary, for something that reconnects us with our higher selves and makes us feel complete, providing us with a sense of belonging and purpose. We've turned to religion, politics, and science to provide us with the solutions to these problems, but all of these methods have failed miserably.

All throughout history, we have sought to answer our internal questions with external answers. In fact, most of us still repeat this misguided search, coming up flat, dead and more frustrated and confused than before.

Religion, although with noble intentions, has caused more harm than good by creating fanatical, self-denying beliefs and ideologies that are open to interpretation. Many of us are realizing this now, and organized religion is crumbling apart quickly.

Science as an answer has merely succeeded in describing *how* the world around us works, explaining what we see and feel (for example, music is a vibration within a gaseous medium), but it can never really explain *why* anything happens. From the Big Bang Theory to Quantum Mechanics, science will describe the process of how the universe came to be without answering our thirst for a deeper meaning that we crave from existence.

Politics is just another human construction we have dabbled in for answers. Constructs such as communism, for instance, have tried to address the issues we face by misguidedly declaring that the system can change the individual without realizing that the system only exists as an illusion. Unless the individual flaws of greed, power-thirst, fear, and so forth are addressed first, these flaws will ruin the entire collective system.

Although many of us are aware of these issues, we individually and collectively continue to carry on our old habits of focusing on the external world for answers and furthering our self-centeredness, materialism, and disconnection from ourselves and the world around us. This obsession with the external world all adds up to an ever-increasing sense of helplessness and insignificance while we watch our leaders fail to acknowledge these problems, or else react in highly dangerous and misguided self-preserving ways.

The Spiritual Awakening Process

While our current personal and global situations may be disheartening, it's a natural result of depriving ourselves of experiencing a wider reality, of failing to expand our consciousness beyond a purely material and individualistic view of ourselves and the universe.

Our vision has always been to provide support, encouragement, a sense of belonging, and a pathway to self-understanding, which our increasingly superficial societies have failed to address and teach us through life. We need to transcend the values of a society that perceives the world in a fragmented and materialistic way and strive towards creating a world that is sustainable, collectively beneficial, and supports the individual spiritual thirst for a more whole, fulfilling life.

This spiritual longing is what gives birth to the lone wolves of life, the sacred fringe dwellers of our planet, the social outsiders of our world, and the Old and Mature in Soul.

To live wisely, love wholeheartedly, and mature fully as individuals and collectively as a species, we must develop our inner world just as much as our outer one. We must learn how to explore the wider realms of our consciousness, appreciating that all life is an interconnected web, an energetic essence that is composed of Spirit, or living energy.

One of the ways we know how to do this is to change our way of thinking, being, and behaving by cultivating spiritual maturity: to follow inner work paths and techniques that lead us towards a more Soulful, caring, and humane way of existing.

It is time to understand that we are spiritual beings that need Soulful sustenance, not soulless automatons who exist solely to indulge our minds and bodies.

To do good, to be good in this world, we must act from a place of inner freedom, of Soulful liberation, of freedom from all of our emotional and mental needs that are tainted by self-gratification, power, and control.

To find freedom, we must go through a spiritual awakening process.

In this book, we'll share with you why and how this process happens, as well as how to retrieve, explore, and communicate with your Soul. This process of inner work, of Soul Retrieval, will help you to live a life infused with meaning, beauty, joy, and love.

"Once the soul awakens, the search begins and you can never go back. From then on, you are inflamed with a special longing that will never again let you linger in the lowlands of complacency and partial fulfillment. The eternal makes you urgent. You are loath to let compromise or the threat of danger hold you back from striving toward the summit of fulfillment."

— John O'Donohue

CHAPTER 1

Crisis and the Spiritual Calling

"You are not dead yet, it's not too late to open your depths by plunging into them and drink in the life that reveals itself quietly there."

— RAINER MARIA RILKE

In our journey towards "civilization," we've found more and more ways to numb and disconnect ourselves from Spirit. We live and work in gated communities, shopping centers, and office buildings, with air-conditioned houses and cars, fences, landscapers, animal controllers, and we spend our leisure time immersed in complex and absorbing technological worlds.

To deal with our Soul starvation, we drown ourselves in prescription medications, alcohol, recreational drugs, consumerism, and other Soul-numbing forms of escapism. We even suffocate ourselves in rigid belief systems that moralize and judge others, promising to alleviate our sense of alienation from life and existential turmoil.

But our Souls are wiser than all of this. There comes a moment in our lives where we grow out of the collective values and ways of living common to our societies. At a certain point in our lives, we realize that the values, attitudes, relationships, and beliefs we've held no longer contribute to the development of who we truly are: our authentic selves.

This awakening, this life crisis, although painful, provides a vital opportunity for us to begin our spiritual journeys toward Wholeness.

Three Different Types of Crisis

In our Western Soul-suppressing societies, most of us experience something known as a "true calling" (or what mythologist Joseph Campbell refers to as *The Call to Adventure*) toward our life purpose, but most of us never truly *hear* or answer to them.

This spiritual calling presents itself in many ways throughout our lives, such as through the death of loved ones, suicidal depressions, illnesses, near-death experiences, divorce, and so forth. But there are three main milestones that call to us the most loudly.

The first calling is what we modernly refer to as the "*quarter-life crisis.*" The quarter-life crisis happens in the first quarter of life: generally, after we finish high school or university. At this time in our lives, we intuitively know that we need to "find" ourselves by leaving behind our family, friends, and hometowns. These people and places formed our juvenile identities as children and teenagers, and we no longer wish to be limited by them.

When I answered this calling, I remembered feeling intense fear and uncertainty. Saying goodbye to everyone and everything you love is a tough and painful task. Indeed, it can be terrifying and gut-wrenching for most people – but we soon discover how crucial a choice is for our happiness and self-fulfillment.

The second significant calling presents itself as a "*midlife crisis.*" This crisis may come in the form of an affair, a divorce, severe job unhappiness, an empty nest, lifeless relationships, endless life dissatisfaction, or disappointment with the way life has gone. Ultimately, the midlife crisis comes at a moment where you've gathered enough wisdom to know that you're not going to live forever.

Most people who experience midlife crises have spent their entire lives raising a family or working in a career. They haven't had the time, or capacity, to ask the essential questions in life. Eventually, something triggers the question, "Is this all there is?"

The third and final calling often arrives as a "*deathbed crisis*" if we didn't answer the previous two callings. The inevitability of our imminent death creates such immense inner turmoil that the light of Consciousness is finally permitted to shine through us. Many hospice workers have confirmed this with me stating that those near death who have accepted this inner calling seem to glow with an internal luminescence.

Although it's better late than never, what a shame that so many people wait until their last moments to taste truth, deep insight, and peace. Some never experience it at all.

We all have to accept our imminent death someday to live life more fully. And the sooner we come to terms with this, the better. But even if we receive this calling late in life, we are still blessed to receive it.

So what happens after we have undergone a life crisis and opened ourselves to our true calling? What can we expect? What do most people experience?

Surrendering to the Hurricane

Listening to your calling and accepting your spiritual awakening often feels like entering a great hurricane.

Suddenly everything you've ever known is ripped away from you and lost in the tempest. The more you struggle, the more you get thrown around mercilessly. But the moment you surrender, you stand in the eye of the hurricane peacefully allowing everything that doesn't serve you to be swept away.

Surrendering is extremely crucial in two ways. Firstly, it allows you to let go of your former limiting self, e.g., all of your beliefs, ambitions, roles, and perceptions of how you were supposed to be. And secondly, surrendering allows you to embody your Soul, that is, all of your deepest longings, dreams, and wildest passions.

It's natural to experience fear and resistance in the face of the hurricane. You'll need to explore deeply what parts of you are creating resistance. There are several ways to do this, but the simplest way (in my opinion) is to write down how the fear feels in your body. What images and memories arise during your process of surrendering? Write down (or even draw) what happened when you were "called" to the spiritual journey and ask yourself questions such as: *where were you when it happened, what catalyzed it, how did your body feel, what emotions arose within you* (and other significant life events connected to this moment)?

As you walk into the heart of your life crisis, you will need to confide in others who are going through similar experiences. Connecting with others can bring a great sense of emotional alleviation and kinship, and you can find many online and local groups dedicated to inner awakenings.

Be prepared to experience immense loneliness as well. After all, surrendering your former worldview separates you from your habitual way of life, including your old anchors, comforts, and even friends or family members. You'll learn how to navigate this process smoothly throughout the rest of this book.

Unfortunately, a large number of people that go through life crises handle their previous responsibilities and commitments in unhealthy ways. You don't necessarily need to quit your job, get divorced, sell your house, abandon your children, and leave your friends to embark on the spiritual path. Instead, starting your journey means becoming more in-tune with your Soul and exploring what is no longer supporting your growth and evolution.

I like to think of this period in life as "spiritual simplification." In other words, what roles, relationships, activities, and possessions are in the way of Spirit flowing through you?

Four Signs You've Had a Spiritual Calling

So how do we know whether we're experiencing a profound spiritual awakening, or just a momentary mood swing or desire to escape from our life responsibilities?

Mythologist and professor Joseph Campbell noted four qualities that accompany the spiritual calling. I've found them to be quite accurate and useful:

1) It's not an avoidance of responsibility

Rather than providing you an opportunity to escape from your problems or burdens, a spiritual calling feels almost ominous. We all have problems we'd rather not face in our daily lives, but if you're experiencing a spiritual calling, you'll somehow sense that an arduous and overwhelming journey lies ahead of you. Despite this, there is a profound desire to embark on it.

2) It's familiar yet frightening

Many describe the sensation as déjà vu or "familiarity" when listening to the voice of their Souls.

3) You feel as though you've reached the end of your current journey

Whether you want to accept it or not, you feel as though your current path has hit a dead end. What once made you happy and excited now feels empty.

4) You weren't looking for your true calling; it found you

Your calling was unexpected and unwanted. But now you face a fork in the road that demands your decision.

Other signs include feeling intensely powerful emotions and even altered states of consciousness or mystical experiences during spiritual awakenings.

Ask yourself, what would happen if you ignored this calling? What emotions arise within you at the thought, and what do they reveal? You might also like to listen to whatever you feel drawn towards, pursue it, and pay attention to whether it feels intuitively right or is driven by undertones of fear. When it's a spiritual awakening or a true calling, you'll feel closer to home with every step.

*"An awakening can happen in a flash.
And in a flash, you are changed forever."*

— **Phil Good**

CHAPTER 2

Spiritual Awakening Stages

As we've seen, going through a spiritual awakening is one of the most confusing, lonely, scary, but also *supremely beautiful* experiences in life.

At its core, the spiritual awakening process is the Soul's cry for freedom. If you listen to its call, your life will be transformed into something meaningful and significant. On the other hand, if you refuse its call, your life may feel like an empty graveyard.

But what happens once you listen to the call? What happens when you have *no choice but to listen?*

While there is no map that clearly marks the wild terrain of awakening, there are what we loosely define as seven main stages of the spiritual awakening process. They can be defined as follows:

Stage 1 – Unhappiness, despondency, and feeling lost

In this stage, you experience the Dark Night of the Soul: a time of confusion, disconnection, alienation, depression, and great unhappiness with life. You are searching for something, but you don't quite know what. There is a great looming emptiness inside of you. This stage either emerges spontaneously or due to a life crisis (e.g., breakup, divorce, death, trauma, illness, major life change, etc.).

Stage 2 – Shifting perspectives

In this stage, you start seeing through the lies and delusions propagated by society. You start to perceive reality in a totally different way. You feel unhappy with life, disturbed by the suffering you see and hopeless to the ills of the world. You no longer see life as you once did in your previous state of complacent unawareness.

Stage 3 – Seeking answers and meaning

There *must* be a point to all this, right? In this stage, you're asking all the deep questions. You are in search of your life purpose, spiritual destiny, and the meaning of life itself. You will start dabbling in different metaphysical, self-help, and esoteric fields in search of answers and truth.

Stage 4 – Finding answers and experiencing breakthroughs

After a lot of Soul searching, you'll find a few teachers, practices, or belief systems that ease your existential suffering. (Beware: falling into spiritual traps often occurs in this stage – we'll explore this topic later in this book.) You'll feel a sense of expansion as old patterns dissolve, and your true nature (Soul) begins to emerge. You may have several mystical experiences or brief moments of Satori (enlightenment) that give you a glimpse into the ultimate nature of reality. This is a time of joy, hope, connection, and awe.

Stage 5 – Disillusionment and feeling lost again

Life is about movement. Within the spiritual awakening process, there is always an ebb and a flow. In this stage, you become bored and tired of your spiritual teachers or practices. You may become disillusioned by the shallow spiritual practices out there and crave for something deeper. You may have even experienced long periods of connection with the Divine, only to become separated again (remember, this is normal). Understandably, you'll feel disturbed and deeply upset by this experience. Additionally, while you may have experienced many mental/emotional/spiritual breakthroughs, they might feel superficial. You crave authenticity and for deep spirituality that permeates your whole life and transforms every part of you. The unhappiness and stagnation you feel will motivate you to go in search for more.

Stage 6 – Deeper inner work

In this stage, you're not interested in dabbling in feel-good spiritual philosophies or surface practices anymore. The abiding pain you feel inside motivates you to do deep inner work. You may become a serious student of meditation, mindfulness, inner child work, shadow work, bodywork, or various other transpersonal practices.

Stage 7 – Integration, expansion, joy

Integration means taking the spiritual lessons you've learned from your inner work and applying them to your daily life. Integration happens both naturally and consciously as a habit in deep spiritual practice. In this stage, you'll experience the most profound and long-lasting changes deep within. Many people experience prolonged mystical experiences and periods of unity with the Divine in the integration phase. Remember that enlightenment is never guaranteed: we can strive for it, but it is ultimately a gift from Life. Nevertheless, profound peace, love, and joy emerge and are felt in this stage. You may feel ready to be a spiritual mentor or role model in your community and pass on your insight to others. Life will become less about you and more about We. Your perspective will expand, and you will start seeing things from the big picture. Above all else, you will feel connected, at peace with yourself, and deeply aligned with life.

It is common to move back and forth between these spiritual awakening stages. Remember that this is not a linear process – you cannot always move from A to B or stage 1 to 2. This is a complex and messy path, so it's perfectly fine if your journey doesn't look like what has been outlined above. Your spiritual awakening process is unique to *you*. But hopefully these stages, in some way, help you to gain your bearings.

"So what is spiritual awakening? It is above all a process; a process of exploration and unfolding; a process of learning and growth, of healing and purification. It involves the whole of our beings and works on all levels, physical, emotional and psychological, as well as spiritual."

— Catherine G. Lucas

CHAPTER 3

Spiritual Awakening Symptoms

Perhaps one of the greatest forms of relief that can come during the spiritual awakening process is understanding the fact that *you're not alone!*

Whatever strange, alarming, disorienting, otherworldly, or plain old frustrating symptoms may be befalling you, it is crucial for you to understand that:

a) You are *not* alone
b) You are *not* going crazy
c) Your pain and frustration is *legitimate*
d) What you're experiencing is *perfectly normal* (in the context of what you're going through)

There is a multitude of bizarre, chronic, and medically unexplainable symptoms that accompany the journey of spiritual awakening. Some are as simple as tingles that keep running up and down your spine. Other symptoms can be as distressing as fits of fainting or full-blown psychotic episodes. We will explore the more severe signs associated with spiritual awakening in a later chapter.

Across the course of your spiritual awakening process, you may have consulted many medical professionals. However, like many undergoing this journey, you may have been met with little to no explanation for your health issues. Your doctor may have mentioned that your concerns were purely psychosomatic (meaning that they are a product of the stressed mind), sent you on a merry-go-round trip through various specialists, or sent you home with half a dozen prescriptions – as if a pill can make everything better.

While some of these chronic issues may, in fact, be purely medical problems that can be solved with scientific healing methods – some of them might extend far beyond the knowledge and understanding of modern medicine. And this might leave you feeling confused, lost, and helpless.

Don't fear. If you're going through something that can't be explained through conventional medicine, *especially if it has occurred in conjunction with your spiritual awakening,* you are likely undergoing a psychospiritual (or psychological + spiritual) malady.

As your Soul undergoes the process of growth and expansion, your life force energy (also known as kundalini, chi, or prana) can intensify and inundate your entire being. On a physical level, this can feel like being short-circuited – which is why many unusual conditions can arise as the body struggles to regain equilibrium.

Below you will find a selection of common physical, emotional, and mental symptoms of spiritual awakening. Be aware that awakening symptoms vary from person to person. In other words, you might experience symptoms that haven't been included on this list, so don't worry if that's the case. Be compassionate with yourself and understand that even if your issue isn't listed below, it is still *legitimate.*

Physical Symptoms

- Amplification of senses, e.g., your sight, hearing, taste, touch, and/or smell becomes intensified
- You discover many food intolerances that you've never seemed to have before (or perhaps weren't paying attention to), e.g., allergies to wheat, nuts, legumes, soy, etc.
- Changed sleeping patterns, i.e., you sleep more or experience more disrupted sleep, often causing insomnia
- Vivid dreams – your dreams become scary, bizarre or intense

- Dizziness – feeling lightheaded as a result of being ungrounded during the day
- Weight change – either gaining or losing a lot of weight
- Changed eating habits – what you once liked eating no longer appeals to you (you may also crave to experiment with other foods that you've never tried/liked before)
- Fluctuations in energy – feeling less energized than you used to or feeling intense bursts of vitality that seemingly come from nowhere
- Decreased or increased sex drive
- Decreased immune function (more illness)
- Tingles up and down your body or in a certain area (e.g., crown of the head, back of the neck, etc.)
- Spontaneous feelings of vibration emanating through your body

Mental and Emotional Symptoms

These symptoms are shared by the majority of people experiencing awakenings:

1. You feel as though your life is false

Everything that you have believed, built, and worked towards seems to be false. Your life doesn't feel as though it's your own. You no longer feel like yourself – nearly everything you once enjoyed no longer brings you meaning or satisfaction.

2. You crave for meaning and purpose

You deeply desire to find the meaning of your life. You have no idea what your purpose is, but you want to find it desperately. There's a sense that something is "missing" inside of you (like a part of your Soul).

3. You begin asking deep questions

Questions such as "Why am I here?" "What's the purpose of life?" "What happens after we die?" "Why do people suffer?" arise. You begin thinking more philosophically. Such profound thoughts may greatly disturb you as you don't know the answers.

4. You realize that a lot of what you've been taught is a lie

You start to see that many of the beliefs, ideals, and values you possess are not your own, but are other people's or inherited from your culture.

5. You feel completely lost and alone

Nothing in your life seems to make sense anymore. You feel as though you're wandering through an endless wilderness. As a vagabond, you feel completely alone and cut off from people. You struggle to relate to those you once felt close to (i.e., your friends, work colleagues, and family members).

6. You see through the illusions of society

Materialism, success, and profit no longer mean anything to you. You start feeling as though you're a cog in the machine of society.

7. You see how unhappy most people are

You awaken to the unhappiness and suffering of others. You may start to explore activism or read more about the human condition. It is tormenting to you to realize how much pain there is in the world.

8. You want to 'purge' your life

You're sick and tired of feeling stranded, depressed, and hopeless. Suddenly, you feel the need to simplify and declutter your life. This could mean cutting ties with toxic people, reassessing your habits, throwing out old things, relocating to a new job or place to live, or even giving away most of what you own.

9. You begin experiencing deep empathy and compassion

As you start paying more attention to the many hardships faced by humanity and nature alike, you develop more compassion. Your inherent empathy is awakened, and you may find it hard to cope with the intensity of your feelings. This is a pivotal point in your inner transformation: you either numb the pain you feel with addictions, or you find healthy ways to accept and express your emotions.

10. You desire to be alone

You crave solitude. In other words, you may have once been socially active, but now you prefer to be socially withdrawn. You also spend a lot of time introspecting and enjoying the silence. At every cost, you try to reduce social contact. At this point on your spiritual path, you may lose touch with many old friends.

11. Conversations seem shallow

When you do talk to people, you feel an acute sense of separation. You realize that very few people are comfortable with talking about passion, emotions, meaning, and the Soul. In conversations, you feel restless and irritated by the small talk. A part of you silently screams, "*Can't anyone wake up and realize what is happening?*" Your distaste for frivolous chit-chat draws you more into solitude. You may become a lone wolf or rebellious free spirit.

12. You want to quit your job

Even though you worked for years getting your degree, establishing your career, and climbing the ranks, you feel nothing but emptiness. Your job no longer provides you the sense of fulfillment that you need. You desperately crave for more.

13. You thirst for authenticity and truth

Being true to yourself becomes your priority. You hate faking and putting on the old masks that you used to wear. You want to be completely authentic. Pretense makes you feel sick to your core.

14. You become aware of your old negative habits

You are painfully aware of your flaws and destructive habits. Within you, a strong urge arises to wipe the slate clean and start over.

15. You experience anxiety and depression

You may go through deep bouts of existential depression or persistent anxiety. The shock of plunging into your awakening leaves you feeling unstable. You may be misdiagnosed with a mental illness. Uncertainty and fear follow you around everywhere.

16. You become more sensitive

Everything impacts you more. You feel the energy of others more strongly, the pain of your loved ones more intensely, and the difficulties in life deeper than ever before. However, at the same time, you feel a gloriously enhanced connection with animals and nature. You start feeling more at home within the natural world (rather than the manmade world).

17. You want to make the world a better place

When all is said and done, you want to leave the world a better place. You start thinking 'big picture.' This longing to make a real impact translates to actively helping others or finding a life purpose that aligns with this desire.

18. You deeply want to understand who you are

Endless questions arise about your identity and your life, for example, "Who am I?" "Why was I born?" "What am I here to do?" "What is the purpose of my existence?" As a result, you begin reading many self-help books and spiritual texts.

19. Your intuition is heightened

Gradually you start to listen to the still, small voice within. You allow it to guide your decisions. Eventually, you start to uncover your hidden gifts and talents.

20. More synchronicity

You start becoming conscious of the many signs and omens that life brings to you. Life becomes much more receptive and interactive with you. Serendipity and déjà vu increase. You may even undergo numerous mystical experiences.

21. You feel more wonder and curiosity

The smallest things start to bring you joy and bliss: a falling leaf, a spider's web, a child's laughter, a puddle. Life is no longer ignored – it is seen as magical, amazing, and beautiful.

22. You start to love unconditionally

As the barriers of the ego breakdown, you begin to love other people without expectations or conditions. You lose interest in drama, conflict, and anything that perpetuates hatred.

23. You see that we are all One

Not only do you intellectually understand that we are all interconnected, but you feel it deep within your bones. You realize that our thoughts and beliefs influence reality and that we are all fragments of one great Whole – that is, Spirit. Having experienced that we are this Oneness, you find peace at last. Sometimes this stage can take years or even an entire lifetime to experience. But you will experience increasingly longer moments of blissful expansion as you progress.

As you can see, the spiritual awakening process is a profoundly life-changing experience. We undergo changes on *all* levels (body, heart, mind, and Soul), and while these shifts can be disturbing at first, they are the beginning of a great inner metamorphosis and adventure. We'll explore the three parts of this spiritual adventure in the next chapter.

"There is a candle in your heart, ready to be kindled.
There is a void in your soul, ready to be filled.
You feel it, don't you?"

— Rumi

CHAPTER 4

The Three Worlds of the Spiritual Journey

Most people in the modern world have resigned themselves to a cliched existence, indulging in endless distractions. They go through life with minimal or pseudo-faith and avoid grasping the emptiness of their lives. They are endlessly haunted by the shallowness of their relationships, neurotic issues, and inescapable loneliness.

And yet there's so much more to us as a species than what we know. You and I carry the most mysterious and magnificent qualities within us imaginable, yet we unknowingly guard and protect the great gift that is our Souls from the world. It's so easy for us to feel meaningless when we perceive ourselves as mere cogs in society's machine. The truth is that we are much more than slaves of 9 to 5 jobs. We are capable of creating deeply meaningful, mystical, and fulfilling lives. We are capable of finding our *true calling*.

For centuries the indigenous peoples throughout the world have known that to explore the depths of the Soul fully, we must venture into a spiritual journey of the unknown darkness within ourselves. In many ancient cultures, there were Elders and Shamans to encourage and oversee these quests toward a deeper spiritual existence. Sadly, in the modern world, we have lost such sacred rites and rituals. Instead, orthodox religion has replaced living spirituality with a theoretical God, dismissing and outlawing personal experimentation and union with the Divine.

Listening to Your True Calling

People have felt this pull toward something greater than themselves since the beginning of time.

Ancient cultures had many stories that served to illustrate the journey to Wholeness or Nirvana. These journeys mythologist Joseph Campbell described as the "*Calls to Adventure.*" A call to adventure is something we all experience at least once in life. When we embark on this adventure, we begin the process of gaining self-understanding and reclaiming our precious Soul gifts.

The archetype of the hero or heroine discovering their true spiritual nature goes back thousands of years. The

Greek's told the story of Orpheus who descended into the underworld to rescue his bride Eurydice from Hades. The Nordic people had their hero-warrior Beowulf, and the Sumerians wrote of Inanna who battled her sister in the dark world. Throughout history, there have been so many stories of individuals who have struggled through hardship to find themselves. These heroes symbolize our spiritual journeys: of leaving everything behind, entering the unknown, encountering countless unconscious monsters, and finally returning home with a sense of renewed fulfillment and wisdom.

The Three Sacred Worlds

"The breeze at dawn has secrets to tell you. Don't go back to sleep. You must ask for what you really want. Don't go back to sleep. People are going back and forth across the doorsill where the two worlds touch. The door is round and open. Don't go back to sleep."

— RUMI

At some point in life, we all experience the call to adventure. Often our journeys start when we experience sudden spiritual awakenings or the Dark Night of the Soul. And usually, without wanting to, we are cast onto the path of Soulful expansion.

Like you, I have wandered these paths and have at times wound up lost and confused. For this reason, I find it useful to map out the spiritual journey in a way that helps the human mind know where it is, and where it will go next. My Andean ancestry speaks of three worlds that we can experience in life: the Upper World (*Hanaq Pacha*), the Middle World (*Kay Pacha*), and the Lower World (*Ukhu Pacha*).

In many traditions and mythologies, these three worlds correspond to the different realms of the Self. The Upper World is the home of Spirit, the Lower World the home of Souls, and the Middle World is the home of the physical body and human ego. Different practices and techniques are used in each of the three realms to help us spiritually mature and rediscover joy, peace, and Wholeness.

Below I'll explore each of these realms with you:

Middle World

Purpose: *Personality development*

In our everyday lives, we function within the middle world. The middle world is responsible for our ego development, and yet many people on the spiritual path ignore this vital element of inner growth. Without developing a healthy personality, our spiritual growth reaches a dead end.

In life, we all begin within the middle world, or physical realm. As children and teenagers, we go through various years of personality change and growth. Finally, as adults, we have all developed unique personalities. However, many of us fail to continue our self-development, getting lost in corporate jobs, and the pursuit of money, status, and fame.

The goal of the middle world path is to develop a healthy personality or ego. Tasks involved in this process include the exploration of core emotional wounds, self-love, and the cultivation of authenticity. A healthy adult ego will be able to love freely, be vulnerable, express creativity, and display empathy towards others.

We cannot develop a healthy personality by using techniques from the Upper or Under World such as meditation or shadow work. Instead, we must use techniques that pertain to ego development and healing such as assertiveness training, non-violent communication techniques, cognitive behavioral therapy, NLP, and other psychological avenues of self-development.

Under World

Purpose: *Soul discovery*

Our Soul is the vital, mysterious, and wild core of our individual selves. It is a unique essence in each of us that goes deeper than our personalities. Think of the Soul as one of many rivers that run back to the ocean of Spirit. Our Souls contain our heartfelt purposes, unique meanings, gifts, and the ultimate significance of our individual lives. To access these deep layers and qualities, we must descend into the Under World of our unconscious minds.

Unfortunately, for thousands of years, our culture has "protected" us from the hardships and dangers of the descent into the Soul. This protection has been done through the establishment of comfortable, predictable, and clockwork lives that revolve around material pleasures and shallow values. In fact, thanks to religious thought, the descent into our Under Worlds has been condemned as "evil" and wayward. Only Shamanic cultures and Western mystical schools like Hermeticism have dedicated themselves to exploring the Under World.

For centuries, the descent into the Under World has been so feared and avoided because it is a perilous journey. There is a reason why Christianity referred to this place as "hell." Within our Under Worlds lie our repressed thoughts, feelings, desires, and even denied gifts. Often when we descend, or *inscend*, into ourselves, we come across many demons, ghastly creatures, and other parts of our Shadow Selves that we've been hiding from or suppressing. The Shadow Self is a part of ourselves that contains all of the repressed, feared, rejected, and wounded aspects of our identities.

However, despite the fact that the Under World journey can be such a harrowing and haunting experience, it is ultimately a life-changing odyssey. Only by descending into our personal Under Worlds can we sincerely come to terms with our true life callings, talents, gifts, and deepest values.

Under World, or *inner work* techniques, include practices that allow us to access our shadow selves and disconnected Soul parts. These practices may include crafts such as lucid dreaming, drumming, shadow work, shamanic trances, inner child work, vision quests, etc.

Upper World

Purpose: *Uniting with Spirit*

The Upper World journey, or that of the ascent, is what we often refer to as Self-Realization.

There comes a moment in our journey between the Middle World and the Under World in which a perfect balance is formed, allowing us to move up into the Upper World. For example, it's much harder to ascend to the Upper World when our unconscious minds are plagued with deep childhood traumas (that stem from the Under World), trust issues (Under World problem), and poor self-esteem (Middle World problem).

We enter the path of ascent into the Upper World when we learn to surrender our ego identification and Soul identification. Ultimately, we not only intellectually understand that everything is One, but we experience it at a core level. At this point, we are free from the illusion of having a separate self. This experience is also commonly referred to as the experience of Enlightenment.

This permanent shift of consciousness is about merging with the Infinite, Divine, Eternal, and Absolute. Techniques used to taste this state of being are often found in the mystical schools of Zen, Kundalini, Taoism, Sufism, and disciplines such as meditation and yoga.

Unfortunately, many people in the spiritual community believe that ascension is all that is needed to experience peace and Wholeness. As a result, the Middle World and Under

World paths have been cast aside as if they don't matter. However, only focusing on your "higher chakras" and cultivating positivity and Oneness with Spirit creates a lopsided individual. When the darker and more practical elements of self-growth are ignored, the result is imbalanced and unhealthy human beings.

Preparing For Your Journey

The spiritual journey to Enlightenment, or Wholeness, is not like climbing a mountain. We rarely start at the bottom and climb to the top. Instead, for most of us, the spiritual journey is like hiking through a beautiful, but perilous range of valleys. Our spiritual journeys alternate between periods of descending and ascending. In one period of our lives, we may cultivate our connection with Spirit, while in other parts of our lives, we may plunge into the Soul to heal core wounds, or the Middle World to develop self-love.

Finally, it is possible and also quite common to get hung up in these valleys. Many of us become lost, distracted, and even forget why we were trying to get to the top of the mountain in the first place. However, with guidance, willpower, and persistence, we can make our way through. That is the purpose of this book.

In the end, you will find that the spiritual journey is like a mystical marriage between the ego, the Soul, and the Spirit. *One cannot exist without the other.* While there is no guarantee that we'll attain this mystical marriage, this spiritual enlightenment, we enter the journey to prepare the soil of our being for grace – as ultimately, enlightenment is a gift from the Divine.

In the next chapter, we'll explore the dark side of the spiritual awakening process. It's important that we honestly face the struggles and dangers inherent in this path with compassion and clarity. Contrary to popular belief, the spiritual awakening process is not always sunshine and roses. In fact, very frequently, it can turn our world upside down and inside out – as you've probably already experienced.

*There is a brokenness
out of which comes the unbroken,
a shatteredness
out of which blooms the unshatterable.
There is a sorrow beyond all grief
which leads to joy
and a fragility
out of whose depths emerges strength.
There is a hollow space
too vast for words
through which we pass with each loss,
out of whose darkness we are sanctioned into being.
There is a cry
deeper than all sound
whose serrated edges cut the heart
as we break open
to the place inside,
which is unbreakable and whole,
while learning to sing.*

— **Rashani Rea**

CHAPTER 5

The Spiritual Emergency

You've gone through a tremendous spiritual awakening. Your life perspective has changed drastically. You're no longer the same person you once were a few years ago. *But something has gone horribly wrong.*

While others on the spiritual path are reveling in their deep insights, you feel suffocated under the weight of an existential crisis.

While others are busy reconnecting with their true life purpose, you can barely function in a job or even get out of bed to shower.

While others feel a deep sense of peace and alignment, you feel like you're on the verge of going crazy or being sucked into the black hole of depression or emptiness forever.

What on earth has happened?

Is it something you did wrong? Is it because you're not worthy? Is it because you're not strong enough?

NO. What you are experiencing has *nothing* to do with your strengths or capabilities. What you're experiencing is something called a spiritual emergency. And as we'll see throughout the rest of this chapter, it's a normal process that *many* people experience during their spiritual paths, and, most importantly, it's not your fault.

What is a Spiritual Emergency?

Before you get too deep into this chapter, it might be worth pausing and checking in with yourself. If you're feeling a bit frazzled or anxious, it might be worth skipping to another chapter and revisiting this chapter when you feel better. The reason why I ask you to pause here is that the information you're about to read in this part of the book may cause you undue stress. We will be dealing with the dark side of spiritual awakening, and to some that can be too scary or *too much* to face right now. So as always, treat yourself with kindness and do a quick check-in. It's perfectly fine to find another chapter within this book to read if you don't feel ready.

With that being said, let's start with a basic definition of the spiritual emergency.

The *spiritual emergency* is a term that refers to a severe crisis that an individual may experience after going through a spiritual awakening. Essentially, a spiritual emergency occurs when the spiritual awakening process speeds up so much that it becomes terrifying and destabilizing to the body and mind. Our inner and outer world may confusingly merge and overlap, intense visions may occur, along with a host of other extreme symptoms.

The phrase "spiritual emergency" itself was a term originally coined by Czech psychiatrists Stanislav and Christina Grof and was expanded in their 1989 book *Spiritual Emergency: When Personal Transformation Becomes a Crisis*. Since then it has increased in popularity, although the term is still relatively unheard of within mainstream spiritual communities. (We want to change that.)

Spiritual emergencies can happen to anyone at any point in life. Those who are not particularly 'spiritual' can experience it just as often as those who are actively engaged in the spiritual path. The common uniting factor is usually that a person undergoes a shock (in the form of illness, family death, major life change, etc.) that triggers the spiritual crisis. The shock is so destabilizing that it throws the whole psyche into a state of chaos.

How long does it last, you may wonder? The spiritual emergency can last anywhere from a few days to a number of years. The process is very much dependent on what kind of environment you live in and how supportive vs. unsupportive it is.

Furthermore, there are two types of spiritual emergency: *the Dark Night of the Soul* and what is sometimes referred to as '*Mystical Psychosis.*'

The Dark Night of the Soul and Mystical Psychosis

The Dark Night of the Soul and Mystical Psychosis can be differentiated in the following ways:

The Dark Night of the Soul is defined as a period in one's life where there is a complete absence of connection to the Divine. Intense existential suffering occurs within this state, and there is an abject sense of emptiness, both within oneself and within the world. Those undergoing a Dark Night of the Soul may feel like the living dead, existing in a lifeless hull of a body that seems to be adrift in a black void of nothingness.

Mystical Psychosis, on the other hand, is a term that refers to the experience of undergoing hallucinations, experiencing paranoia, seeing visions, and otherwise losing touch with reality. Those undergoing Mystical Psychosis may be hospitalized, committed to a mental health ward, or heavily medicated. Many theories surround Mystical Psychosis, with the most prominent being that mental illnesses (such as schizophrenia) are actually profound spiritual initiations. When the Mystical Psychosis is thwarted, and not valued for its potential spiritual implications, it can evolve into a mental illness that is pathologized and reinforced by society.

Historically, we can see Mystical Psychosis play out in figures such as St. Teresa of Avila, Vincent Van Gogh, Nietzsche, and Carl Jung. The Dark Night of the Soul, on the other hand, can be seen in figures such as St. John of the Cross, Eckhart Tolle, and Mother Teresa.

The main difference between these two types of spiritual emergency seems to be the direction that energy flows. With Mystical Psychosis, the energy seems to flow *upward and beyond* into higher realms of Spirit or Consciousness. On the other hand, with the Dark Night of the Soul, the energy seems to flow *downwards and in* – or into the realms of the Collective Unconscious and Soul.

It is possible to have a little bit of Mystical Psychosis paired with the Dark Night of the Soul (and vice versa). It's even possible to have *both* equally. But most people tend to experience only one type of spiritual emergency.

Within these two main categories exist ten experiences that Christina and Stanislav Grof identified as the main varieties of spiritual emergency. They are:

1. Peak experiences
2. Kundalini awakening
3. Near-death experiences
4. Past-life memories
5. Psychological renewal
6. Shamanic crisis
7. Psychic opening
8. Communication with spirit guides and channeling
9. Close encounters with UFOs
10. Possession or obsession states

These ten varieties of spiritual emergency don't necessarily stand alone. Often they mix and combine in confusing, even terrifying ways.

St. Teresa and St. John

We'll now examine two fine examples of historical figures who experienced Mystical Psychosis and the Dark Night of the Soul respectively. We'll delve into their illuminating stories below:

St. Teresa of Avila, a Spanish mystic born in 1515, entered the Carmelite Order as a young woman. Since a young age, she had suffered from severe and mysterious fainting fits that would often leave her semi-conscious, in pain, and paralyzed. What is interesting about Teresa is that she underwent the longest and most intense spiritual emergency on record. In her own words, she described one particularly grave attack:

> *"I had an attack which left me insensible for almost four days. They gave me the Sacrament of the Extreme Unction and in every minute of every hour thought I was dying ... For a day and a half a grave was left open in my convent, waiting for my body."*

Thankfully, Teresa's suffering finally gave way to ecstatic raptures upon seeing a particular statue of Jesus one day while walking down a corridor in the convent. She was thirty-nine years of age. From then on, her seizures turned into mystical experiences of Union with the Divine. Teresa is a fine example of a historical figure who underwent a spiritual emergency in the form of mystical psychosis. Her story shows us that, often, such severe unexplainable physical maladies, when seen through the spiritual framework, are preparation for deep and powerful spiritual transformation.

St. John of the Cross, on the other hand, suffered the second (and more prevalent) type of spiritual emergency: the Dark Night of the Soul. In fact, he is the creator of this very term which he originally used as the title of his book, '*Noche Obscura del Alma.*'

Born just thirty miles and twenty-seven years apart, John of the Cross and Teresa of Avila can be thought of as 'twin saints.' John even considered Teresa to be his spiritual mother. He too experienced a spiritual emergency, but one that was not characterized by painful seizures but a catastrophic sense of inner disconnection from the Divine.

St. John's story, like all life stories, is complex, but what is important to know is that he met Teresa on his travels shortly after being ordained. Teresa, being impressed with his zealous nature, asked him to join her reformation of the Carmelite Order. Through a stroke of destiny, John agreed and became a confessor in one of her nunneries.

But the journey quickly turns dark. In 1577, the traditional Carmelites who had rejected and outlawed Teresa's reformed branch of the Order kidnapped and imprisoned John. Trapped in a poorly ventilated windowless cell so low he couldn't stand up, with a diet of only bread and water, John was cast into the abyss of the Dark Night of the Soul. He was also tortured repeatedly during this period and repeatedly fell ill due to his severe malnourishment.

Tormented by such a horrific circumstance, John fell into the pits of despair. But, thanks to the kindness of one particular prison guard, John was given writing materials with which he used to record his great work, *The Dark Night of the Soul*, by the light of a three-inch hole high in the wall. In his own words, he describes the depths of suffering that can occur during the spiritual emergency:

> *"The Divine assails the soul in order to renew it and thus to make it Divine; and, stripping it of the habitual affections and attachments of the old man, to which it is very closely united, knit together and conformed, destroys and consumes its spiritual substance, and absorbs it in deep and profound darkness. As a result of this, the soul feels itself to be perishing and melting away, in the presence and sight of its miseries, in a cruel spiritual death, even as if it*

had been swallowed by a beast and felt itself being devoured in the darkness of its belly, suffering such anguish as was endured by Jonas in the belly of that beast of the sea. For in this sepulchre of dark death it must needs abide until the spiritual resurrection which it hopes for."

Such words highlight the profound suffering that accompanies the Dark Night of the Soul. The feeling of inner darkness can be so consuming that it can feel like there's no hope, no light, and no end to one's misery.

But don't be alarmed. There is *always* hope, even amid the most unspeakable suffering. As John writes in *The Dark Night of the Soul:*

"It now remains to be said that, although this happy night brings darkness to the spirit, it does so only to give it light in everything; and that, although it humbles it and makes it miserable, it does so only to exalt it and to raise it up; and, although it impoverishes it and empties it of all natural affection and attachment, it does so only that it may enable it to stretch forward, divinely, and thus to have fruition and experience of all things, both above and below."

Thankfully, St. John escaped after nine months of imprisonment.

As we can see, the Dark Night is a period of death before rebirth, crucifixion before resurrection, night before day, destruction before creation. It is the metaphorical caterpillar cocoon we enter to unite with our True Nature. But before we taste the dawning light, before we feel the bliss of expansion, we must go through the process of darkness and dissolution. What is old must be destroyed for the new to come about. And this process can be long, arduous, harrowing, and distressing. But in the end, it's worth it. Furthermore, there *are* ways to make the process flow more smoothly. We'll explore these practices a little later. But first, let's explore the key signs unique to the spiritual emergency.

Signs You're Experiencing a Spiritual Emergency

"Cosmic love is absolutely ruthless and highly indifferent; it teaches its lessons whether you like/dislike them or not."

— JOHN LILLY

If you think you might be going through a spiritual emergency, you have my deepest love and support. This is likely one of the most painful, disorienting, and scary experiences you will ever go through – but please know that it does end, and it is worth going through.

The Spiritual Awakening Process

Below, you'll find several signs commonly experienced during spiritual emergencies:

1. You find it impossible to cope with everyday tasks (like going shopping, showering, cooking, keeping up with the bills, etc.)
2. You can't hold down a job due to your intense sensitivity
3. It feels like your whole world is crumbling around you
4. You struggle to sleep properly and may experience night terrors
5. Your inner and outer world blur confusingly
6. You regularly experience a rollercoaster of emotions
7. You may experience strange hallucinations (e.g., images, sounds, physical impressions)
8. Your grasp on the real and logical is weak (resulting in psychotic-like symptoms)
9. You may believe, at some point, that you're the reincarnation of enlightened figures like Jesus, Buddha, Mary, etc. (this is called *ego-inflation* and

is a result of Universal Consciousness overlapping with your own personal consciousness)

10. You may experience vivid past-life flashbacks
11. You feel strange sensations in your body (e.g., vibrations, shivers, heat, burning)
12. You've developed a medically unexplainable illness
13. You experience more synchronicity or meaningful coincidences than ever before
14. You feel like you're being sucked into a different dimension or black hole
15. You feel like you're going crazy

Of course, this list is not exhaustive. I'm sure there are many other symptoms out there that I've neglected to include. So if you're experiencing something that hasn't been mentioned here, please know that it is real and it is valid.

Also, those who work in the mental health field may have a thing or two to say about the above list of symptoms. Yes, it's true that many of the above symptoms overlap with 'bipolar disorder,' 'manic-depression,' 'schizophrenia,' etc.

However, life is rarely black and white. We'll explore this important overlap a little later – and what it means for you.

Why Do Spiritual Emergencies Happen?

Honestly, there is no one single known reason *why* spiritual emergencies happen. The cause, I suspect, is unique for everyone.

But here are some explanations:

1. **It's your destiny** – by experiencing an accelerated spiritual awakening process, you are about to learn some profound lessons, work through a tremendous amount of karma, and transform into the most illuminated version of yourself possible in this lifetime.

2. **Your conditioning was particularly strong** – conditioning meaning the beliefs, ideas, habits, and patterns adopted from your parents and society. To break through these forms of conditioning and dissolve them (so that you can experience a conscious 'upgrade'), you had to undergo a particularly intense spiritual awakening.

3. **You're a gifted shaman, priestess, healer, or "walker between worlds"** – part of your spiritual

awakening process involves connecting you with the forces of the unconscious mind or "spirit realm" which you have not yet learned to navigate (hence why you're experiencing a spiritual emergency).

4. **You're dealing with past karma** – in some belief systems it's believed that we deal with unresolved trauma from our past lives in this lifetime – and that may take the shape of a spiritual emergency to help you purge ancient patterns and develop a 'clean slate.'

5. **You're more sensitive** – we all have various levels of sensitivity, and those who undergo a spiritual emergency may be more sensitive and empathic than others. This may explain why the would-be spiritual awakening turns into a spiritual emergency; it's simply too overwhelming for those already sensitive to life. Again, there is no way of proving this, but it is one theory that you might like to mull over.

Take a few moments to think about which theory you resonate with (if any). You'll be able to uncover the true reason for you based on how your physical and emotional landscape responds. Which description triggers something inside of you? Whichever theory you strongly react to is likely the correct explanation for you.

However, regardless of what explanation you resonate with, it's vital to stress here that **it's crucial to give your spiritual emergency a purpose.** As Friedrich Nietzsche wrote, "He who has a why to live for can bear almost any how."

Are You Experiencing a Spiritual Emergency or Mental Illness?

"Breakdowns precede breakthroughs."

— LEE LOZOWICK

You might be curious to know whether the spiritual emergency is actually just a fancy name for a psychotic break, manic-depressive episode, or other severe mental illness? This is a tough question to answer, as there's no black or white "yes" or "no."

Those who undergo spiritual emergencies are often committed to mental health wards – either forcibly or voluntarily. As author Catherine G. Lucas, founder of the UK Spiritual Crisis Network writes:

"There are literally thousands of people who have been through the mental health system who have not had the spiritual aspect of their experience honoured. The spiritual dimension has been completely overshadowed by the interpretation given to their experience by the medical model."

These unfortunate (even tragic) individuals have been forcibly injected with high doses of medication, held against their will, shunned by their families, rejected by society, and labeled by the system as pathologically mentally ill.

Although it can be argued that the mental health system (which is a fundamentally flawed institution) is only doing what it knows best, a psychiatric unit isn't the safest place for a person who is undergoing a spiritual emergency.

Those who *don't* end up committed usually buy into the pathologizing perspective of the mental health system – there simply aren't many other alternatives. They may be diagnosed with a mental illness, instructed to take medication every day to keep their symptoms under check, and shooed away like a herd animal until their prescription expires – and the cycle continues.

While I'm not at all trying to imply that it's a good idea to get off your medication if you suspect you've undergone a spiritual emergency, it is good to be educated and have more options. Sometimes a small amount of medication is necessary to help prevent complete system shutdown – and that is a blessing the medical world offers us. But it's not the only solution.

As Lucas writes in her book *In Case of Spiritual Emergency*, the process of being tossed through the medical system can be severely traumatizing and actually prevent us from fulfilling the natural cycle of the spiritual emergency – and reaping its rewards:

"Overall, perhaps the greatest danger of ending up in a hospital, and certainly the saddest aspect, is that the opportunity for healing and growth, for living a fuller, richer, more awakened life, can be irretrievably lost. The natural process of renewal, as the psychiatrist John Weir Perry called it, can be totally thwarted. Both the trauma of hospitalisation and the over-use of medication can have this effect. And once the process has been stopped in its tracks it can be difficult, if not impossible, to retrieve."

Furthermore, having our mystical experiences dismissed as being purely 'psychotic,' 'borderline,' or 'schizophrenic' not only denies the spiritual validity of what we're going through but also adds an unnecessary element of fear and terror to the experience. This fear and terror can be profoundly crippling and can make the whole experience much more difficult than it really needs to be.

Thankfully, there are some in the medical field (typically Jungian and transpersonal therapists) who understand the spiritual significance of symptoms that would otherwise be dismissed as "ramblings of a crazy mind." I encourage you to seek these sort of professionals out, and if you have the energy, ask them if they are familiar with the spiritual emergency. You can also visit the spiritual emergence network if you need to find someone close to you. (Please see the references section at the end of this book for more information.)

Roger Walsh, an Australian professor of psychiatry, philosophy, and anthropology, is one such figure in the medical field who validates the spiritual emergency. He calls it the "developmental crisis":

"Developmental crises are periods of psychological stress that accompany turning points in our lives. They may be marked by considerable psychological turmoil, sometimes even of life-threatening proportions. These transitions can occur spontaneously, as in adolescent and midlife crises, or can be induced by growth accelerating techniques such as

psychotherapy and meditation. These crises occur because psychological growth rarely proceeds smoothly. Rather, growth is usually marked by periods of confusion and questioning or, in extreme cases, disorganization and despair."

So is it a spiritual emergency or psychosis?

We need to understand that sometimes, experiences can be both/and – not either/or. In this situation, you may be experiencing *both* a spiritual emergency *and* some form of psychosis – but they shouldn't be seen as two distinct things.

As Lucas writes, "*… I am not interested in trying to distinguish between so-called psychosis and spiritual emergency. I take the view that it is all the psyche's attempt to heal and move towards wholeness, that each experience is potentially spiritually transformative.*"

What you're going through is valid and important, and you need to seek out those who will help you see your spiritual emergency through a positive lens, not a negative one. This book is a crucial place to start.

How to Cope With the Spiritual Emergency

"There is a crack, a crack in everything. That's how the light gets in."

— LEONARD COHEN

I write "cope" instead of "cure" because the spiritual emergency has a mind of its own. What we're dealing with here is a force of nature, a Divine movement of energy that cannot be tampered with without adverse effects (such as those stuck in the mental health system carousel).

There is no six-steps-to-happiness process here. I wish there were. I would so love to provide that for you. But that would be disingenuous and disrespectful to the process you're going through. Perhaps what is most important to take away from this chapter is that **your suffering has a purpose and your experiences are spiritually valid.** If there's anything you remember from this book, I hope it's this.

While there is no formula for healing, as every journey is different, there are some practices you can try which have helped those on a similar path before you.

Please take these forms of advice very slowly and stop at any time if you feel worse:

1. Stop meditation and practice mindfulness instead

Many people who undergo spiritual emergencies simply cannot tolerate meditation. Why? Meditation can be very dissociating if you're not grounded strongly in your body. (And those undergoing Mystical Psychosis or the Dark Night struggle to keep their grip on this plane of existence!)

Meditation can also open up certain doorways within the mind and encourage the influx of unconscious material. For a person already being bombarded with images and visions from the deep mind, this can be profoundly destabilizing.

During this difficult time, it's better to practice mindfulness. Mindfulness means consciously paying attention to the present moment. When we are mindful, we are fully engaged with our body and senses. Tuning into your sense of taste, touch, smell, sight, and hearing can help to bring you back down to earth and into your body.

Try to practice mindfulness a little bit every day. Wash the dishes mindfully and feel the cold water against your hands. Hang up the clothes mindfully, and listen to the birds chirping outside. Eat mindfully and notice the different textures and flavors filling your mouth. You get the picture!

2. Seek out earth energy

Try to bring the energy of the earth into your daily life. As you may or may not already know, the earth's energy is deeply grounding and nourishing. If you need help anchoring yourself into this realm, go outside and dig in the soil. Get your arms elbow-deep in the dirt. Plant some seedlings in your backyard. Take care of a pot plant indoors. Sit underneath a tree and feel the ground underneath your feet. If need be, bring a heavy stone to bed so you can literally become grounded.

3. Carry something comforting with you

If you're going through particularly scary or painful bouts of anxiety or depression, carry around something that comforts your inner child. This may be a stuffed toy, a blanket, a crystal, a photograph, or anything that you associate with safety. One of my favorite 'comforters' is a heat pack that I warm up in the microwave (it comes out smelling like home-cooked bread).

4. Temporarily stop your spiritual practice

To some, this may sound drastic, but the spiritual emergency isn't something to be trifled with. It's important to understand that some types of spiritual practice can intensify Mystical Psychosis and the Dark Night of the Soul. In the interest of your sanity, it might be best to put your practice aside for a while and focus on mundane tasks. If you absolutely cannot do without some form of spiritual nourishment, try earth-centered approaches to spirituality, like spending time in nature. Ultimately, whether you follow this advice or not is up to you and your situation. But definitely consider the possibility that your spiritual practice might be detrimental to your wellbeing right now.

5. Eat hearty food

During the spiritual emergency, it's tempting to ignore what we eat (simply because we're too preoccupied or have no energy). But please, try your utmost to eat at least one hearty meal a day. When I say hearty, I mean the food needs to be grounded. Focus on root vegetables like sweet potatoes and beetroots. If you're vegetarian or vegan, you might consider temporarily changing your diet to include organic free-range meat – desperate times call for desperate measures!

6. Find the purpose in your suffering

Examine again the five potential reasons why spiritual emergencies happen (see the beginning of this chapter). Why do *you* think you're experiencing a spiritual emergency? Listen to your heart and let the answer emerge. You'll know you've found the truth when you feel full-body shivers, a sense of peace and clarity, or a sudden "aha!" lightbulb moment. If you can't find any satisfactory explanations mentioned in this chapter, you may like to pray to the Universe/God/Goddess/Soul or whatever to help you find the meaning. This prayer doesn't have to be religious, it can be spiritual or secular. Simply communicate your intention and notice any signs that arise in the next week.

7. Exercise (even just for a few minutes)

Depending on your situation, you may like a full-body catharsis (like high interval training) or a gentle activity like walking. Pay attention to your needs. Exercise is vital for mental health and general physical wellbeing. It also connects you with your body and the surrounding world, which is important during the spiritual emergency.

8. Understand your own hero/ine's journey

One of the best ways to put your spiritual emergency in context is to follow your own Hero/ine's journey. The Hero's Journey is composed of 12 stages and was first popularized by mythologist Joseph Campbell. Here are the stages that have been adapted by Christopher Vogler in his Twelve Stage Hero's Journey:

1. **The Ordinary World** (*everyday life before the spiritual awakening/emergency*)
2. **The Call to Adventure** (*an inner call to voyage into the unknown – the beginning of the spiritual awakening/emergency*)
3. **Refusal of the Call** (*fears and concerns that hold us back from accepting the call*)
4. **Meeting With the Mentor** (*meeting a wise friend, guide, teacher, or helper who is an integral part of your journey of transformation – this can be an inner or outer force*)
5. **Crossing the First Threshold** (*the initial step into the unknown*)
6. **Trials, Friends, and Foes** (*undergoing struggles and meeting those who support you and reject/hurt you*)

7. **Approaching the Innermost Cave** (*reaching the central crisis of the journey*)
8. **The Ordeal** (*undergoing the plunge into the dark, the great abyss, the great death and rebirth*)
9. **Reward** (*emerging on the other side triumphant, reborn, and with new gifts and strengths*)
10. **The Road Back** (*journeying back to the ordinary world*)
11. **Resurrection** (*meeting the final ordeal/test*)
12. **Return With the Elixir** (*bringing the gifts and lessons learned back to everyday life*)

Why use the Hero's Journey? Essentially, the Hero's Journey is a pattern (or archetype) that can be found in all cultures, religions, and periods since the dawn of humanity. In every book, movie, and life journey, you'll find different versions of the same underlying odyssey. By exploring your own journey, you'll be able to gain a sense of clarity, understanding, and hope. Ultimately, the core purpose of this activity is to understand that *your journey has a beginning and an end, and the pain you're experiencing will not last forever.* Furthermore, there's actually a light at the end of the tunnel, which can be seen after the 'death and rebirth' stage.

I encourage you to reflect on the stages you've gone through and are currently experiencing in the Hero's Journey and write them down in a journal. If you need more help understanding what each stage means, do a Google search for "the hero's journey."

9. Avoid stressful situations and reduce your responsibilities

Stress exacerbates any form of spiritual emergency, and holding onto many responsibilities tends to produce a lot of underlying anxiety. If you have many projects or people needing your energy, it might be best to drop the vast majority of your commitments. The spiritual emergency demands your energy and attention, and getting lost in workaholism is a recipe for disaster. Therefore, try to simplify what you can and give yourself some much-needed breathing space.

10. Seek support

Yes, in the midst of psychosis it might be necessary to be medicated and hospitalized (low doses of medication are generally better than high doses during spiritual emergencies – but I am not a medical professional, so please listen to your own common sense). But generally, if your experience doesn't require 24/7 observation, it's best to seek out a therapist or spiritual counselor who is familiar with the notion of spiritual emergencies.

I've previously recommended transpersonal and Jungian therapists within this book, however, please do your own research and ask them whether they know about spiritual emergencies. Seeking therapeutic support is a wise choice, and you can visit the Spiritual Emergence Network to see if there are any professionals near you (see the references section at the end of this book for a link to the website). Alternatively, you can just do a Google search and include the name of your city while searching for "spiritual counselors" or "transpersonal therapists." If worse comes to worst and you can't find any within a reasonable distance, you can always try someone who does online Skype sessions.

Why am I not recommending the support of friends or family members? The reason why is because usually those close to us have no understanding of the spiritual emergency and tend to be negatively conditioned by medical institutions. In other words, it's much more likely that they'll get spooked by your experience (as they're comparing it to the "old" you) and actually invalidate the experience rather than validate it. This is not a hard and fast rule, and some friends or family members *are* mature and may have gone through similar experiences. So try to use your gut instinct when making a decision, and above all, put your wellbeing first.

Most importantly, do not let *anyone* try to convince you that what you're going through is "nothing but crazy" or that your visions/insights are "irrelevant." Denying the spiritual element of what you're going through is monumentally short-sighted and detrimental to your wellbeing. You have the right to honor your experience and find meaning in it, as indeed it *is* meaningful.

The Spiritual Emergency is a Sacred Process

When all is said and done, the spiritual emergency may be terrifyingly life-altering, but it is a sacred process of clearing out the old and welcoming in the new.

While the medical world may pathologize you and the mundane world may reject you, you are not crazy, you are not alone, and your experiences *do* have profound spiritual meaning and significance.

Take care of yourself, dear soul. You are doing the best that you can, and you are so courageous for walking this path. *Thank you for your immeasurable bravery.*

In the next chapter, we'll be examining a topic that underpins all spiritual emergencies: Soul Loss. Get ready to do some inner deep diving.

*"Paradoxically, we achieve true wholeness
only by embracing our fragility
and sometimes, our brokenness."*

— Jalaja Bonheim

CHAPTER 6

Are You Experiencing Soul Loss?

In our society, there is a mysterious phenomenon occurring known as "Soul Loss" arising in all people of all ages, genders, races, and backgrounds.

Indigenous people have known about the occurrence of Soul Loss for millennia, and understand it as the result of an inner fragmentation caused by unawareness, a traumatic experience, or, an intense shock to the mind and body.

When we experience Soul Loss, a part of our psyche "hides" or shuts away, hindering us from expressing and experiencing our true potential and Wholeness as human beings. Often, entire aspects of our psyches are completely blocked out or repressed.

When people think of Soul "Loss," it's easy to believe that parts of our Soul become lost mistakenly – but this is not the case. Rather, Soul Loss literally means "*losing touch with the Soul.*" Our Souls are completely whole, undivided, and intact; they can never be destroyed or harmed because they are an expression of Spirit itself. Instead, it is our psyches or psychological egos that become fragmented. So when a part of our conscious self goes into hiding to form a blockage in the unconscious mind, we refer to this as Soul Loss because we lose connection to our Souls. In other words, it is psychological trauma that prevents us from fully opening ourselves to the Soul and its sacred source of power, love, and strength.

While Soul Loss may sound uncomfortably familiar to many of us, this experience is usually temporary, and with the proper Inner Work, these lost elements of ourselves can be actively reintegrated into our lives.

What Is Soul Loss?

"Consider the following as possible symptoms of your spiritual homelessness: chronic illness; listlessness; unconscious consumerism; self-distractive behavior; egocentricity and narcissism; nightmares; images of gloom and doom during waking hours; dullness of eyes; perpetual dissatisfaction; addictive behaviors; heartlessness; hopelessness; chronic rigidity; inexplicable agitation, rage, or grief."

— JEFF BROWN

In the shamanic perspective, Soul Loss occurs when the Soul travels off into other realms, or alternate realities, sometimes being possessed by spirits. When these parts of our Souls aren't recovered, such ancient cultures believe that we can't find inner completion or Wholeness.

Before psychology, this explanation was the only way primal cultures could explain such a phenomenon to find ways to treat it – and it was helpful at the time.

These days, however, Soul Loss is the rule rather than the exception. As individuals, we lose our Soulful energy every time we identify with our egos; every time we seek to feel Whole again through addictions, stimulation-seeking, dogmatic beliefs, conditional relationships, and workaholism.

Aside from our incapacity to feel Whole, when we experience Soul Loss, we begin experiencing feelings of weakness, fatigue, depression, anxiety, and emptiness. We just know that *something* is missing from our lives – but many of us struggle to discover what exactly is missing. To understand Soul Loss as a detachment, or disconnection, from the most vital parts of who we are, is known in psychology as "dissociation" – a root of many mental maladies.

The Psychology Behind Soul Loss

Once we recognize our Souls (or Consciousness) as energy, anything that creates a reduction in this energy will result in listlessness, moroseness, and depression.

To create an imbalance within the psyche, individual parts of the personality (e.g., the shadow self, inner child, etc.) must make themselves independent and thus escape the control of the conscious mind.

Psychologist Carl Jung understood this process as relating to our "psychic libido." Jung proposed that our personalities are composed of different "complexes" (or parts of our sense of self). The primary one of these complexes responsible for control over all the others is our "ego" – which is the mental image we have of ourselves, or what we *believe* ourselves to be. When one of our inner "complexes" escapes the control of our ego and is repressed within the unconscious mind, our conscious energy ("psychic libido") is weakened and incomplete. As the unconsciously repressed complex naturally seeks to be made conscious, it will find every opportunity it can to rise to awareness. But we can't tolerate such an intrusion, so we will repress, deny, and avoid any of these parts that make us feel uncomfortable. The result is a psychological imbalance that shatters our natural Wholeness.

So what provokes one of our psychological complexes to emancipate itself and become a tyrannical usurper of consciousness? Often the answer is that identifying with something harmful or experiencing a trauma of some kind creates this phenomenon.

An extreme example might help us understand better:

Imagine that a young child is molested or abused. In order to cope with this horrendous experience, the child escapes by dissociating or detaching herself from the situation. In the process of protecting herself, the child unconsciously creates various alter egos or entirely different personalities within herself as a defense mechanism. In psychology, this is treated as "multiple personality disorder" (now known as Dissociative Identity Disorder). It is easy to understand how tribal cultures would have perceived this as a loss of the Soul. But essentially, psychological dissociation is nature's way of protecting ourselves against intense trauma and loss by blocking these wounding situations out of awareness.

But Soul Loss, or psychological dissociation, is not limited to these extreme cases and can be found in different degrees in most people. Addictions, eating disorders, identity disorders, post-traumatic stress, depression, codependency, narcissism, low self-esteem, and adjustment disorders are all common causes for (and symptoms of) Soul Loss in our superficial, fast-paced, materialistic modern societies that are mostly devoid of all sense of sacredness.

A young woman who dreams of being an artist but has to live up to her parent's expectations of being a doctor will lose a little bit of connection to her Soul, ignoring an essential part of her being. Or suppose the young woman does go ahead and follow her dream of being an artist, but deep down, she still depends on her parent's love and approval. She then either blames them so that she can avoid taking responsibility for pursuing her passion, or she develops depression because she is not accepted by them. This story might sound familiar to you.

But all is not doom and gloom. Thankfully, there are many ways of finding Wholeness again. We'll explore these methods in the next few chapters.

Signs You Might Be Experiencing Soul Loss

There are a variety of physical, psychological, and spiritual symptoms connected to Soul Loss. When we experience

Soul Loss, parts of our psyche "hide away" or disassociate from us and the result is a loss of Soulful energy – the very vitality of our lives. This loss of primal energy prevents us from experiencing true vitality, joy, happiness, and fulfillment. Sometimes Soul Loss can last for a whole lifetime, resulting in the development of a self-destructive individual who we often refer to as a "lost soul" in our English language.

To recover these lost parts of ourselves, and to become balanced, Whole, and centered once again, we must first identify the symptoms of Soul Loss within us. Below you will find some of the most common symptoms. How many can you relate to?

- Memories and parts of your life have been blocked out.
- You experience strong periods of depression.
- Parts within you feel missing or broken.
- You experience a general numbness towards life.
- You are constantly plagued by feelings of anxiety or fear.
- You go through long periods of insomnia.
- You feel lost or incomplete.

- You feel like a "different person" after a shocking or traumatic life event.
- You feel stuck or incapable of overcoming a certain issue in your life.
- You feel disappointed with life.
- You feel as though there are multiple "selves" within you.
- You try to escape by turning to alcohol, drugs, sex, television, or excessive busyness.
- You feel unworthy of being loved.
- You are experiencing a Dark Night of the Soul.
- You want to find your purpose and meaning in life.
- You feel like your daily life is meaningless and task-driven.
- You avoid feeling vulnerable and keep others at a distance.
- You long for Wholeness and a sense of belonging.
- You sometimes feel that you're not in control of yourself.
- You constantly feel mentally or physically fatigued for no medical reason.
- You thirst for authenticity and complete acceptance of yourself.

To be healthy, to feel Whole, and to live a harmonious life, you must recover the lost vital parts of yourself by learning to live a life of balance, authenticity, and self-love.

Finding the fragments of your psyche that are lost and reintegrating them into your life helps you to reconnect to the innate Wholeness and vitality that is your Soul.

Next, you'll discover how to reintegrate the lost elements of your psyche through the practice of Inner Work so that you can live a mindful and Soul-centered existence.

"Ultimately, all soul loss is a separation from our own divinity, from our natural self that always lives in grace. This self doesn't reveal its face until we confront our wounds, have the courage to rewrite our limiting soul contracts, and begin the hero's journey toward healing."

— **Alberto Villoldo**

CHAPTER 7

How to Practice Soul Retrieval

When I was a young boy, my Abuela (grandmother), would do something very strange. Every time I fell or hurt myself, she would quickly grab me by the head and whisper into my ear a prayer. This prayer was to call my Soul back.

I was always puzzled by her sudden prayers until she explained to me why she did them. As I mentioned previously, in shamanic cultures, Soul Loss is understood to be a spiritual illness. In other words, when a part of our psyche fragments, all kinds of emotional, physical, and mental diseases occur from the diminishment of our life force energy. It is therefore seen as vital for parts of the psyche to return to Wholeness again.

To some extent, we all experience a level of Soul Loss in our lives. Many people don't feel Whole. Ask yourself this question, "When was the last time I felt absolutely Whole and complete?" If you're like most people, that time may have been back in childhood. Perhaps you can't even remember a time when you ever felt Whole.

Because of the mass phenomenon of Soul Loss, issues such as addiction, chronic sickness, diseases, abusive relationships, crime, shopaholism, and workaholism run rife in our society. All of these issues stem from Soul Loss.

Common causes of Soul Loss include:

- Any form of abuse, e.g., sexual, emotional, physical or mental
- An event of prolonged grief, pain, and fear that made you feel helpless or impotent
- Deep-seated addictions, e.g., substance dependency, food addiction
- A near-death or out-of-body experience
- Being forced to act against your morals
- An experience of intense rejection or abandonment
- Witnessing the unexpected death of someone
- A sudden and shocking accident
- Entering a relationship without strong boundaries (resulting in an unhealthy relationship and losing your personal power)
- Religious conditioning
- Anything that caused extreme fear within you

In this light, it's easy to think of Soul Loss as something bad that has happened *to* us. However, here, it's essential to realize that Soul Loss is in fact, *a gift* – it is something that has happened *for* us.

In the same way that you become unconscious when you're experiencing immense amounts of physical pain, your Soul is wise and knows your conscious limits. Your Soul knows what your psyche can and can't handle, so parts of your psyche hide away as a survival mechanism to protect you from feeling the fullness of pain.

This splitting of the psyche only becomes an obstacle when the pieces aren't actively retrieved. This fragmentation of the psyche is what leads to chronic depression, suicidal tendencies, post-traumatic stress syndrome, addictions, immune deficiency problems, and grief that refuses to heal.

However, the retrieval of these psychological pieces is not the end of the work. We must then learn how to integrate them back into our lives so that we can recover the vital power, potential, and energy they possess.

Without being able to connect with our Soul, we don't feel Whole. Instead, we feel weak, depressed, anxious, or empty. We feel as if something is missing, and we'll fill that emptiness with anything we can.

However, once we've recovered these lost pieces, we can experience the following benefits:

- Feeling more grounded in our body and more solid
- Feeling energized, awake, and more alive
- Greater presence in the world
- More awareness of our choices, behaviors, and decisions
- Lightness and joy
- Awareness of huge amounts of energy that we didn't know we had
- Mental clarity and a new sense of hope
- Physical well-being and less sickness
- A sense of purpose and renewed direction
- Deeper sleep
- Overcoming addictive dependencies (drugs, food, work)
- A new-found Wholeness and sense of belonging

To undergo Soul Retrieval, you will benefit from having an experienced guide. However, shamans are not the only healers that can perform Soul Retrieval. Other healing practices such as hypnosis, witchcraft, and psychoanalysis all have methods for integrating split-off or lost parts of the self. It is also possible to retrieve the lost parts of your psyche yourself, which we will explore a little later.

The Soul Retrieval Journey

Soul Retrieval refers to the ability to retrieve access to the Soul through the integration of lost or repressed psychological pieces.

To retrieve a psychological part, shamans typically enter trance states with their clients. This altered state of consciousness helps them to journey into one of the three spirit worlds (generally the Underworld) where they are accompanied by spirit helpers with the intent to retrieve a particular part of the psyche. They narrate the whole journey to the client or visualize it through active imagination.

In these Soul Retrieval journeys, they encounter strong, often harsh energies that manifest themselves through the archetypal images of monsters, reptiles, dragons, and other dangerous beasts. These are the Guardians of the Psyche, or in psychotherapy, they are known as defense mechanisms of the mind. The shamans must overcome these with the help of their spirit helpers so that they can persuade the psychological part to come back.

Once the shaman has retrieved the psychological part, they reintegrate it together with the client. This process of reintegration is usually done energetically (by blowing the energy into the body), through a ceremony, or through cognitive tools (such as inner child work or Gestalt therapy).

Soul Retrieval is only successful if the person who is healed consciously decides to use this newfound energy to cultivate healthy choices that support their Wholeness. The process of healing is a two-way dance!

If you've done a lot of Inner Work, Soul Retrieval might come right at the end of your journey. On the other hand, Soul Retrieval might be the first step you take to help you rediscover your Wholeness.

Soul Retrieval Techniques

While you will benefit from having a skilled healer assist with your Soul Retrieval, it is also possible to perform Soul Retrieval on yourself. However, please note that this is much more challenging, and not everyone manages to retrieve and especially reintegrate parts of their psyche.

There are many Inner Work practices out there that can help you to retrieve the repressed parts of your psyche. Here are a few examples:

- Visualization
- Self-hypnosis
- Automatic writing
- Art therapy
- Breathwork
- Somatic healing
- Dream analysis
- Oracle cards
- Silence and contemplation
- Mindfulness meditation
- Sacred ritual
- Surrender and non-resistance
- Exploration of core beliefs
- Discovery of core wounds
- Self-love
- Spirit Guide discovery and guidance
- Discovering your power place
- Inner child work
- Self-inquiry
- Shadow work

This is by no means an exhaustive or comprehensive list as there are so many Soul Retrieval techniques out there. Therefore, because there are so many methods to choose from, we'll help to make this path easier for you by sharing the three most powerful Soul Retrieval practices we've encountered in the next few chapters. These three methods are *inner child work, self-love,* and *shadow work.*

As Jungian psychoanalyst and poet Dr. Clarissa Pinkola Estés writes in her book *Women Who Run With the Wolves*:

A healthy soul shines through the persona on most days and blazes through on others. Where there is gross injury, the soul flees. Sometimes it drifts or bolts so far away that it takes masterful propitiation to coax it back. A long time must pass before such a soul will trust enough to return, but it can be accomplished. The retrieval requires several ingredients: naked honesty, stamina, tenderness, sweetness, ventilation of rage, and humor. Combined, these make a song that calls the soul back home.

Here, Estes succinctly defines the most crucial aspects that all Soul Retrieval journeys must include, that is; naked honesty, stamina, tenderness, sweetness, ventilation of rage, and humor. And within the three Soul Retrieval paths that we'll explore next, all six of these precious qualities are harnessed, honed, and cultivated to a profoundly healing degree.

"Reclaiming and championing your wounded inner child allows you to heal and integrate your ego. Once integrated, your ego then becomes the source of strength that allows you to explore your wonder child: your essential self. Paradoxical as it may seem, your ego needs to be strong enough to let go of its limited defensiveness and control. You need a strong ego to transcend ego. To give a crude example: the ego is like the booster rocket that puts you into orbit. Your soul takes over from there, operating in the unlimited expanse of outer space. The relationship between your wonder child (Soul) and your wounded child (Ego) must be healed before you can connect with your essential self. Once you've done your ego work ... you're ready for full self-actualisation."

— John Bradshaw

CHAPTER 8

Inner Child Work

The first method of Soul Retrieval is something known as inner child work.

No matter how big or small, all of us have experienced some kind of trauma as children.

These wounds could vary from having your favorite stuffed toy thrown in the trash, to being abandoned by your best childhood friend, to being physically or emotionally abused by your parents.

Inner child work is a vital component of Inner Work because it reconnects us with a wounded element of ourselves: the child within. When we reconnect with this fragmented part of ourselves, we can begin to discover the root of many of our fears, phobias, insecurities, and sabotaging life patterns – this is where the authentic healing happens!

Likely, you'll be surprised by what you discover through inner child work. Instead of simply looking at a symptom of your pain, you'll go right to the core and reveal when a fear, phobia, or certain life pattern began.

Types of Childhood Trauma

Firstly, it's important to understand that there are different types of childhood trauma. These include the physical (including sexual), emotional, and mental variety. When childhood trauma is severe or repeated enough, it results in Soul Loss; this is why inner child work is a major Soul Retrieval technique.

However, not all childhood traumas result in Soul Loss — but they do result in a wounded psyche. When our psyche is harmed, the result is a life spent struggling with problems such as depression, anxiety, low self-esteem, phobias, destructive behavioral patterns, and even chronic illnesses.

Examples of childhood trauma could include:

- Being hit or smacked by your parents/grandparents/caretakers
- Having an emotionally unavailable parent who withheld affection

- Being "punished" through kicking, shaking, biting, burning, hair pulling, pinching, scratching or "washing out the mouth" with soap
- Being the recipient of molestation, shown pornography, or any other type of sexual contact from a parent, relative or friend
- Being the child of divorce
- Being given inappropriate or burdensome responsibilities (such as caring for your parents)
- Not being fed or provided a safe place to live
- Abandonment (or your caretakers leaving you alone for long periods of time without a babysitter)
- Emotional neglect, i.e., not being nurtured, encouraged or supported
- Being deliberately called names or verbally insulted
- Denigration of your personality
- Destruction of personal belongings
- Excessive demands
- Humiliation
- Car accidents or other spontaneous traumatic events

There are many more examples of childhood trauma out there, but I just wanted to provide you with a few to give you an idea of what inner child work helps to heal. It's also important to remember that our parents weren't the only ones responsible for provoking childhood trauma — our grandparents, brothers, sisters, extended family members, family friends, and childhood friends may have also played a part.

What is Inner Child Work?

This leads us to the definition of inner child work:

Inner child work is the process of contacting, understanding, embracing, and healing your inner child. Your inner child represents your first original self that entered into this world. S/he contains your capacity to experience wonder, joy, innocence, sensitivity, and playfulness.

Unfortunately, we live in a society that forces us to repress our inner child and "grow up." But the truth is that while most adults physically "grow up," they never quite reach emotional or psychological adulthood. In other words, most "grown-ups" aren't adults at all. This inability to reach true adulthood leaves most people in a state of puerile fears, anger, and traumas that fester away in the unconscious mind for decades.

Sadly, denying and snuffing out the voice of the child within causes us to accumulate heavy psychological baggage. This unexplored and unresolved baggage causes us to experience problems such as mental illnesses, physical ailments, and relationship dysfunction.

In fact, it could be said that the lack of conscious connection to our inner child is one of the major causes of the severe issues we see in today's society. From the brutal way we treat the environment, to the cruel way we talk to ourselves, we have become completely separated from our original innocence.

25 Signs You Have a Wounded Inner Child

At this point, it's vital that you examine how wounded your inner child may be. Pay close attention to the following signs: they will help you learn the general extent to which your inner child has been wounded and the level to which you might feel unsafe in this world. The more signs you say "yes" to, the more inner child work needs to take precedence in your life:

- In the deepest part of me, I feel that there's something wrong with me.

- I experience anxiety whenever contemplating doing something new.
- I'm a people-pleaser and tend to lack a strong identity.
- I'm a rebel: I feel more alive when I'm in conflict with others.
- I tend to hoard things and have trouble letting go.
- I feel guilty standing up for myself.
- I feel inadequate as a man or woman.
- I'm always driven to be a super-achiever.
- I consider myself a terrible sinner, and I'm afraid of going to hell.
- I constantly criticize myself for being inadequate.
- I'm rigid and perfectionistic.
- I have trouble starting or finishing things.
- I'm ashamed of expressing strong emotions such as sadness or anger.
- I rarely get mad, but when I do, I become rageful.
- I have sex when I don't really want to.
- I'm ashamed of my bodily functions.
- I spend too much time looking at pornography.
- I distrust everyone, including myself.
- I'm an addict or have been addicted to something.
- I avoid conflict at all costs.

- I'm afraid of people and tend to avoid them.
- I feel more responsible for others than for myself.
- I never felt close to one or both of my parents.
- My deepest fear is being abandoned, and I'll do anything to hold onto a relationship.
- I struggle to say "no."

If you answered yes to ten or more of these statements, working with your inner child should be at the top of your priority list. If you answered yes to five or more of these statements, it would be wise to seriously consider reconnecting with your inner child. We'll explore how to do that next.

How to Work With Your Inner Child

"Hold the hand of the child that lives in your soul. For this child, nothing is impossible."

— PAULO COELHO

Learning to work with your inner child isn't about becoming childish again, it is about reconnecting with your *childlike* side. There is a big difference between these two states of being.

While being childish means behaving in an immature or naive way, being childlike is living in a state of curiosity and open-heartedness.

We all have the capacity to experience our original childlike innocence; that period in our lives when we saw the world with openness and wonder. To remove the guilt, shame, fear, hatred, self-loathing, and anger that we carry with us, we have to heal the child within. To recover from Soul Loss, we must show the inner child that we care for it. And to do this, we must earn the trust of our inner child through love and self-nurturing.

Your inner child is an essential part of the intricate patchwork that makes up your identity. When you ignore or deny your inner child, s/he is doomed to wither away within the dark vaults of your unconscious mind. However, when you face your inner child, life becomes lighter, and a huge burden is lifted off your shoulders.

Still, that's not to say that inner child work is easy per se. There is so much pain to be faced when working with this neglected part of you. But there is also tremendous joy and vitality to be experienced.

One of the most exciting and miraculous aspects of inner child work is that often hidden gifts and aptitudes that we've long lost touch with emerge. Not only that, but many of our relationships improve, our addictions/habits lessen or fade away, and our connection with our Soul deepens. Finally, self-love and acceptance are possible as we open our arms to our original self. I'm not saying that you will experience *all* of these benefits *right away*, but you'll undoubtedly experience deeper and deeper changes in your life so long as you're committed!

Before we examine how to work with your inner child, I want to remind you that these exercises are not intended to replace therapy, programs, or groups for the inner child/child abuse. If you've gone through child sexual abuse, severe emotional abuse, or have a mental illness, seeking professional help is crucial. This chapter is meant to be an empowering supplement.

Finally, if you experience strange or overwhelming emotions while practicing the advice below, *please stop immediately.* Seek the help of a professional counselor before proceeding. Remember that everything takes time. The practices below are not quick fixes. They're not sparkly wands that will immediately make everything better. But they will give you the basic tools you need for feeling safe, secure, and protected at a core level. I truly hope you find something below that will nourish you and your relationship with your inner child.

Here are six of the most powerful ways to perform inner child work:

1. Speak to your inner child

Acknowledge your inner child and let her know that you're there for her. Treat her with kindness and respect.

Some self-nurturing things you could say to your inner child include, for example:

- I love you (completely and unconditionally).
- I hear you (and I am receptive to you).
- I'm sorry (for the way I have treated you in the past, or for not listening).
- Thank you (for being there for me).
- I forgive you (for anything you believe you've done in the past).
- I will stay here and support you.
- I love you just the way you are.
- I'm so glad you're here.
- I want to take care of you.
- I want to spend time with you.
- I want to hear your thoughts and feelings.

- It's okay to feel sad and scared.
- It's okay to be yourself.
- You're allowed to say no.
- You are so special to me.
- You have so much to offer the world.
- I believe in you.
- I will protect you against harm.

You can say these affirmations as many times as you need, whenever it is necessary during the day. You might even like to use a special voice when saying these affirmations, such as the voice of a wise old man or a loving mother. Furthermore, feel free to create your *own* loving affirmations! The list above will help you get started, but often the most powerful affirmations organically arise from your deepest needs. Make a habit of talking to your inner child, and s/he will become your greatest friend.

2. Look at pictures of yourself as a child

Go through old photo albums and rediscover the face of your younger self. Let that image burn into your brain because it will serve you well throughout the rest of your inner child work. You might even like to put photos of yourself next to your bedside table, in your wallet, or around the house just to remind yourself of your inner child's presence.

3. Recreate what you loved to do as a child

Sit down and think about what you loved to do as a child. Maybe you liked climbing trees, playing with toy blocks, cuddling toy bears, or eating warm porridge. Make time to include whatever activity you enjoyed doing as a child in your present life.

Through inner child work, people have told me that they've connected to sides of themselves that they never even knew existed as adults. Most adults who commit to this work, for example, are amazed at how silly, innovative, and playful they can be. There are so many discoveries to make during inner child work, and they can be genuinely life-changing.

When it comes to recreating what you loved to do as a child, you might need to schedule in "playtime" and allot a time in your schedule. You know how life gets as an adult (that's right, *busy*), so make sure you trick your adult brain and make space to bring this work into your life consistently. Exploring any embarrassment or resistance you feel toward this work will also be useful. Remember, it's completely normal to feel a bit foolish at first, but it's important to keep an open mind.

4. Write a letter *to* your inner child

Imagine that you're a wise, gentle, and loving wizard or fairy godmother. Imagine that you want to adopt your inner child. As you write the letter, tell your inner child how much you love them and want to spend time with them. Write in a way that makes you feel safe, cared for, and understood. Here's an example of a letter I have written to my own inner child:

Dear Little Ale,

I'm so happy you're born. I am here to protect, love and care for you. I want to help you feel loved and accepted for who you are. I want to show you that it's safe to be heard, to feel, and to be seen. I want you to feel like you will always have a home with me no matter what. I want to help and guide you every step of the way. I love you so much.

Love,

Fairy Godmother Aletheia

If you feel emotional during this process, that's okay and actually a good thing. Let yourself cry and be proud of your courage to express how you truly feel.

5. Write a letter *from* your inner child

Using your non-dominant hand (in order to bypass your logical side of the brain), write yourself a letter from the perspective of your inner child. For example, if you are usually right-handed, use your left hand to write. Using your non-dominant hand will help you get more in touch with the feelings of your inner child. Here is an example of my own inner child speaking to me:

Dear Godmother,

I want to find home. Please protect me. I don't want to feel alone anymore.

Love,

Little Ale

You can write back and forth between your Wizard/Fairy Godmother self and your little self. Creating this conversation often reveals a lot of surprising and buried emotions and new information.

6. Do an inner journey

One of the most powerful ways to reconnect with your inner child to heal childhood traumas is to undergo an inner journey.

For beginners, I recommend two types of inner journeys: those done through meditation, and those done through visualization.

To experience these inner journeys, it's essential that you first gain the trust of your inner child through the previous activities. Once you have developed a strong connection to your inner child, you can then ask it to reveal what earlier life circumstances created the trauma you're struggling with today.

Here's how to conduct your own inner child meditation or visualization journey:

How to Do a Meditation Journey

Connecting to your inner child through meditation is a passive process: just breathe deeply, relax, allow yourself to witness your thoughts, and ask your question. For example, you might like to ask, "Dear inner child, when was the first time I experienced trauma in my life?"

Allow yourself to witness the thoughts that rise and fall within your mind. Your inner child may or may not decide to reveal the answer to you. Remember to be patient, loving, and accepting. If your inner child doesn't want to reveal the answer, embrace that. It's important that your inner child feels safe, secure, and ready.

You might like to repeat your question every now and then if nothing of significance arises inside of your mind. Remember that your inner child can communicate with you through words, thoughts, feelings, and even memories. This process can take anywhere from a couple of minutes to 1 hour or more.

Furthermore, remember that your inner child quite often communicates with you through symbolic and allegorical language, so take any unearthed memories with a grain of salt. For example, a memory of getting tortured by your parents might symbolically reveal how your inner child felt around them – it's not necessarily an accurate depiction of what actually happened. If, however, you are concerned by any apparent memory that has emerged, seek the help of a trained trauma therapist. They will help you determine whether such a memory is real or false and what to do next.

Tips: To do the inner child meditation journey, you'll need to have experience meditating. Learning to witness your thoughts can take a lot of practice, so if you're not used to meditating, you might struggle with this technique (thus, you might like to focus on visualization instead). Additionally, if this practice is hard for you, you might want to play some soft ambient music in the background to facilitate and deepen your meditation journey.

How to Do a Visualization Journey:

A more active way to reconnect with your inner child and earlier life traumas is through visualization.

To connect with your inner child through visualization, you must create a "power place" or safe place. This safe place will enable your inner child to feel comforted, held, and supported, which will facilitate more back-and-forth engagement. To create this nourishing place, visualize a beautiful garden or any place in which you feel safe, empowered, and whole. After entering your power place, you can then invite your inner child to speak with you.

Here are a few steps you can take for discovering your power place:

1. Relax, close your eyes, and breathe deeply.
2. Imagine that you're walking down a dark but friendly staircase.
3. At the bottom of the staircase is your power place (or safe place). In this place, you feel safe, secure, and supported.
4. Feel the anticipation arise within your body as you descend to the bottom of the staircase. What will your power place look like?
5. Once you have arrived at the bottom of the staircase, open the door that appears in front of you. Look inside. This is your power place. What does it look like?
6. Spend a bit of time in your power place. Soak it in. What does it look like, smell like, and sound like? For example, your power place might be next to the ocean, within a botanical garden, or inside of a children's nursery.
7. After you have acquainted yourself with your power place, imagine that your younger self has entered, perhaps through a door or waterfall. If you want to

connect with your baby self, you might discover them resting in a patch of grass or in a cot.

8. Say hello, hug your younger self (ask permission first), and make them feel at home.
9. When you're ready, ask your inner child your question, e.g., "When was the first time you ever felt sad or scared?" You might like to phrase the question in child-like terminology.
10. Await their response. Keep in mind that your inner child may interact with you through words, thoughts, images, or even telepathically.
11. If your inner child isn't prepared to speak to you yet, honor their decision. Refrain from trying to force or persuade them to talk to you. Remember that gaining and maintaining trust is essential.
12. Make sure that you hug them (ask permission), thank them, and tell them how much they mean to you.
13. Say goodbye to them.
14. Leave your power place and ascend up the stairs.
15. Return to normal consciousness.

These are basic steps, but they provide a good outline of how to perform an inner child visualization journey.

As children, we perceived the world very differently from our adult selves. Because of this, many of the things we presently assume never hurt us as children may have left deep scars within our psyches. This difference between our adult perception and childlike understanding is why it's important never to make assumptions about your inner child.

Through inner child work, you can learn to grieve, heal, and resolve any sources of trauma you've been unconsciously holding on to for years. This type of Inner Work can liberate you and allow you to reconnect with your Soul, find your purpose, and experience authentic joy and fulfillment.

In the next chapter, we'll explore the second major Soul Retrieval technique for reconnecting to your inner center: *self-love*. Self-love perfectly complements inner child work and can be practiced not only alongside it but at *any* moment of the day.

*"You have to love yourself
because no amount of love from others
is sufficient to fill the yearning that
your soul requires from you."*

— Dodinsky

CHAPTER 9

Self-Love

*A*ll throughout our early lives, we were taught how to read, write, calculate, build, destroy, theorize, study, and analyze life. We were taught how to say "please" and "thank you," as well as what was acceptable and unacceptable to others and society at large. But most of us were failed to be educated in one essential dimension of life: self-love – a path of direct communion with the Soul.

For most of us, self-denial and self-sacrifice were two of the main values taught in our childhoods, and they continue to be emphasized as the markers of a "kind, caring, and worthy human being" to this very day.

Unfortunately, these two values teach us nothing more than the profound emotional and psychological pain of being a self-imposed martyr with no real understanding of genuine self-love.

So what is the result of not being taught the value of self-love in childhood, and adopting the socially acceptable guise of martyrdom (that is, giving up who we fundamentally are) later in life? The result of not practicing self-love is *depression, bitterness, anxiety, resentment, and grief.*

The truth is that without first learning how to love ourselves, we cannot truly know how to love others. This maxim applies to each and every being on the planet regardless of race, gender, religion, or culture. To use a basic analogy, how can an empty cup be used to quench the thirst of another? It is impossible. First, the cup must be filled to feed others. Likewise, we can't give love if we haven't first filled ourselves with love.

Initially, coming to terms with the fact that we were brainwashed to behave as self-sacrificial martyrs can be hard to stomach. But the good news is that with time and persistence, we can learn how to heal ourselves. In essence, we can teach ourselves to become doctors of the Soul; healing our wounds, curing our sicknesses, and maintaining optimum health through the development of self-love.

What is Self-Love?

So what exactly is self-love, you might be wondering? In short, self-love is the forgiveness, acceptance, and profound respect for who you are deep down – all your beautiful and hideous parts included. When you love yourself, you can take care of yourself, honor your limitations, listen to your needs, and respect your dreams enough to act on them. When you love yourself, your happiness, health, and fulfillment are all of the supreme importance because you realize that without loving yourself, you will never be able to love others genuinely.

The Profound Benefits of Self-Love

Self-love illuminates, enhances, and deepens every aspect of life. Other than helping you to reconnect with your Soul, here are some of the *many* benefits of learning how to love yourself more:

- More tolerance of your flaws and weaknesses
- More self-confidence
- More self-forgiveness
- Healthier mindset (and less self-sabotaging thoughts)
- Improved ability to discover and fulfill your personal destiny
- Increased love, acceptance, and compassion for yourself

- Increased love, acceptance, and compassion for others
- Improved relationships
- Improved friendships
- Improved work-life
- More authentic connections with people
- Enhanced joy and gratitude for life
- Increased playfulness, creativity, and spontaneity
- More self-trust
- Healthier and wiser choices
- Increased access to new opportunities
- Improved mental health (and less anxiety + depression)
- Deeper access to one's true spiritual path

But remember, *self-love is a process*. It's normal to alternate between self-love and self-hatred. It's normal to go through ups and downs. However, the more you practice embracing yourself each and every day, the more you'll be able to deal with whatever life throws at you.

So how do we do that, exactly? How do we practice self-love?

How to Practice Self-Love

Below you'll find some powerful self-love practices to assist in your process of Soul Retrieval. These practices will nurture you on all levels (the body, heart, mind, and Soul):

1. Change your diet

Swap processed, fatty, and sugary foods, with whole, unprocessed, and low-fat foods. So much research has shown the link between food and the mind. Eating the wrong types of food is a sign of self-neglect and contributes to physical, emotional, and even mental illnesses. Try slowly cutting out junk food and experience the immense benefits!

2. Explore the core beliefs that keep you small

Core beliefs are the central unconscious convictions we have about ourselves that we developed in childhood. Common negative core beliefs include: "I'm bad," "I'm worthless," "I'm unlovable," "I'm irredeemably broken," "I'm ugly," and so on. There are many ways to uncover and change your core beliefs. But one of the most simple, direct, and powerful practices out there for exploring your core beliefs is something known as *mirror work*. Quite simply, mirror work involves using a mirror to examine the hidden thoughts and feelings that you have about yourself.

To begin this practice, stand in front of a mirror in your house and designate at least ten minutes to stand alone and undisturbed with yourself. Then, simply look at yourself in the mirror in a gentle, steady way. Gaze into your eyes and pay attention to any emotions and thoughts that emerge. Pay attention to inner dialogue that sounds like the following: "I look so ugly," "This is stupid," "There's something wrong with me," and notice what type of thoughts and feelings you keep having. Then, enfold your body in a hug, look at yourself and say, "It's okay, I am here for you, I accept you" (or whatever feels the most loving and authentic to you). Afterward, write about your experience in your journal. Reflect on the thoughts and feelings that kept arising during your mirror work. What themes frequently emerged? What unspoken beliefs or assumptions are behind them? Asking these simple questions will help you to uncover your core beliefs.

3. Get 7-8 hours of sleep every night

Getting less than the recommended 7-8 hours of sleep every night lowers your immunity, contributes to chronic fatigue, moodiness, depression, anxiety issues, and chronic pain (or fibromyalgia). Aim to go to bed around 10 pm and rise at 6 am. (Also, ensure that you set a stable bedtime to ensure consistency.) You will feel the difference mentally and emotionally!

4. Be your own advocate and stand up for yourself

Being your own advocate means exploring what your needs are and respecting them, which is a form of self-love. *What is non-negotiable or an absolute deal-breaker in your life? What are your deeply cherished values? What are your boundaries?* We all have them. Standing up for what you believe in is a form of self-respect.

In order to be your own advocate, you need to explore what is making you feel unhappy, depressed, or overwhelmed in your life. *What lines are being crossed? In which areas do you feel used or taken for granted? What makes you feel unsafe?* You might like to explore these questions in your journal.

Remember that being assertive about your needs and values isn't a synonym for being obnoxious. You don't need to be loud, angry, or emotionally reactive to be an advocate for yourself – that approach will backfire very quickly. Instead, healthy assertiveness is about honoring yourself while at the same time, being respectful towards others.

Some mantras or affirmations that you might like to repeat to yourself to practice healthy assertiveness include:

- "I calmly and firmly honor my needs."
- "I respect my needs gently and assertively."
- "I allow myself to say no clearly and respectfully."
- "I honor my needs, values, and feelings always."
- "I create clear and consistent boundaries that protect my energy."
- "I have the right to defend my needs and desires."

You can also take these mantras/affirmations, adjust them, and create some of your own!

5. Explore your mental traps

Low self-esteem is often a result of false and unrealistic thought patterns that are deeply ingrained within us. These patterns are composed of mental traps such as assumptions, beliefs, comparisons, desires, expectations, and ideals about ourselves and others. One great way to explore your mental traps is by keeping a daily diary of your private thoughts and feelings. Ask yourself, "what am I feeling?" and "why?" You might like to counteract any negative thoughts you come across with questions such as, "can I find evidence to the contrary?" and "do I know that's 100% true?"

6. Treat yourself like you would your best friend

Often, we are our own worst enemies. So that we can override and undo this harmful inner programming, we need to treat ourselves with compassion and consideration just as we would with a best friend.

Ask yourself the following questions: *How close are you with yourself? Do you give yourself pep talks, just like a best friend would? Do you treat yourself to fun and exciting activities that you love? Are you there to hold your own hand when things get messy?* If your answer is "no" or "rarely" or even "sometimes" it's time to do things differently. You are with yourself 24 hours a day, 365 days a year. Make time each day to do something, anything, no matter how small, to remind you of this sacred connection that you have with yourself. (The rest of the suggestions on this list are a good start!)

7. Welcome solitude into your life

When we don't make space in our lives to be alone, it's easy for us to burn out, become chronically stressed, and alienated from ourselves, others, and life itself. Each day, strive to make time for yourself to unwind, relax, and reflect, *alone*. This might include spending just five minutes outside and drinking a cup of tea as you watch the clouds in the sky.

Or you may choose to spend twenty minutes in solitary meditation. Whatever you have time for right now, remember that solitude is a direct pathway to your inner world. Solitude gives you insight, perspective, and reinstates harmony in your life.

8. Meditate for self-awareness

Becoming self-aware is a crucial skill in life, a gift that allows you to identify your self-destructive patterns of thought and behavior, and find more peace and balance in everyday existence. Meditation, although frustrating and seemingly pointless at first, is an immensely powerful practice that helps you to become more self-aware and therefore increase your self-love. If you're a beginner, aim for 10-15 minutes each morning first thing. Try a simple meditation such as breath-awareness or sound-awareness. All that these meditations require is to focus on either your rising-and-falling breath or the sounds around you. Whenever your mind wanders, gently draw your attention back to your breath or the sounds in your environment. Repeat this practice for the entire length of your meditation.

It's normal to feel frustrated and alarmed by how chaotic your mind is when first meditating (we all experience this). But through time, your mind will become quieter, your heart will open, and you'll gain more direct access to your Soul.

9. Identify toxic people in your life

Toxic people are individuals who drain your energy and continuously harm you in some way. You can tell you're in the presence of a toxic person if you frequently feel fatigued, wretched, or unhappy after spending time around them. Toxic people are also known as *energy vampires,* and they tend to be judgmental, manipulative, clingy, double-crossing, ruthless, aggressive, controlling, deceitful, self-pitying, and self-destructive. While it is important to understand that such people act out from a place of pain, it's also vital to take care of yourself. Learning to distance yourself from (or even cut away) those who hinder your self-growth is a challenging, but necessary step on your journey of healing.

10. Seek supportive companions

Supportive people encourage us, uplift us, and inspire us. These people have often obtained a high level of self-love, and because of their ability to respect themselves, they can easily respect and love others. Often it is not necessary to seek these people out as we naturally gravitate towards them on our paths! However, it always helps to instigate friendships and connections with these types of people as they can help us out in dark periods of our journeys.

11. Learn to trust your intuition

Our unconscious minds are oceans of wisdom, understanding, and insight. Intuition, that mysterious inner guide we all have, is a manifestation of this vast untapped world within us. Learning to trust your intuition will help you to live a life true to yourself and your deepest needs, and reconnect with your Soul. In order to begin listening to your intuition, keep a journal of all your intuitive insights during the day. Test the validity of one or two of these insights the next day and record the results. The more you pay attention to the quiet voice within, the more accurate and perceptive it will become.

12. Take a walk or jog each day

Walking or jogging is not always possible, but regular exercise has an immense benefit on your body, mind, and Soul, proving that you are actively taking care of yourself. Try to schedule in thirty minutes of active time each day in an enjoyable environment such as a home gym or local park. Choose your setting wisely, and you might just be motivated to do *more* exercise (or at least be consistent)! Even if you suffer from a chronic health condition or disability that limits your mobility, it's still possible to do mild, gentle, and brief forms of exercise. Make a daily habit out of conscious movement, and it will soon become second-nature to you.

13. Stop spending so much time on social networks

Did you know that the average American adult checks their social media accounts at least once every waking hour of the day? In total, that equals about 4 or more hours each day spent on websites and apps such as Facebook, Twitter, Snapchat, Instagram, and Pinterest. *And that number is increasing.*

In truth, we waste so much of our time on social media. Often we are motivated by the ability to obtain "likes," "shares," "followers," and "friends," constructing a cyber alter-ego that craves for social acceptance and esteem. For this reason, social media is generally an unhealthy environment to expose ourselves to each day. Many studies have shown its detrimental effects on our health, including an increase in depression and low self-esteem. Try turning off and unplugging your digital devices regularly, opting for real-world interaction instead.

14. Use color psychology

Colors are said to significantly impact our psychology (hence the field of "color psychology"). After all, every color is a specific vibration. People who replace their black, gray, and dull-colored clothing with brighter alternatives notice an interesting difference in their mental states. Wearing light blue, for instance, stimulates feelings of openness, and yellow, for example, boosts optimism. Dull colors like khaki, granite, and charcoal, on the other hand, are all associated with feelings of apathy, aloofness, pessimism, and despondency. Try introducing new colors into your life – particularly those associated with the heart (pink and green) – and pay close attention to the impacts they have on you.

15. Make time to explore your passion

What drives you, fires you up, and fills you with a sense of accomplishment? When we suppress our needs to cater to other's needs, we often lose sight of what truly makes us happy in life. Many of us abandon our dreams at an early age. We then go on to live meaningless lives of drudgery and commit to socially approved pursuits that don't fulfill us (such as having a prestigious career, big house, nice car, perfect family, etc.). It is vital, therefore, to ask yourself, "What is *my* passion?" Think about what you loved doing as a child and use that as a springboard for further discoveries. Remember, passions are not static, and they can evolve with us. Whether painting, writing, dancing, designing, building, or whatever excites you – pursue it – even if on the sidelines!

16. Focus on reducing sources of stress in your life

Prolonged stress contributes to so many illnesses in our lives, so it is essential to learn how to reduce and deal with it when it comes. Often stress can be reduced by simply reducing the high expectations we have of ourselves, other people, and situations in life. Remembering that we are all flawed (and that's okay) is a simple but effective way of letting our anxiety go. Stress can also be reduced by practicing many of the things I have mentioned in this chapter, e.g., having a healthy diet, getting 7-8 hours of sleep per night, targeting negative thought-patterns, and so forth.

17. Accept your flaws and difficult emotions

It is important to come to terms with the fact that you are imperfect – there is no denying it. However, by accepting your flaws and inner demons, the doorway to self-growth is opened. So embrace your warts and pimples, don't run away from them. Likewise, learn how to celebrate your strengths! Keep a journal of affirmations and honestly list each day every thing, great and small, that you appreciate about yourself. Balance is essential.

As spiritual teacher Jeff Foster puts it:

"Don't judge your sadness, your depression, your feelings of unworthiness so quickly, and don't judge the sorrows of another, for you really don't know what's best for anyone, for you really don't know more than life itself. That which you reject (in another or in yourself) may actually be much-needed medicine, a misunderstood teacher, inviting you to a self-love deeper than you ever thought possible. It may be a threshold guardian, a gatekeeper of a forgotten kingdom!"

Instead of seeing your guilt, jealousy, anger, fear, and sadness as a terrible curse, see them as *opportunities to grow*. Realize that everyone struggles with these universal human emotions. We *all* feel insecure at times, and that's perfectly okay.

18. Laugh at yourself

Not in a mocking or self-derisive way, but as a friend would. Be good-natured towards yourself and find humor in the strange little things you say, think, and do. When you stop taking yourself so seriously, your heart opens, and you become more receptive to experiencing self-love and inner Wholeness.

19. Realize that you are fundamentally worthy

Most of us equate failures in our lives with us *personally* being failures. We need to remember that if we outsource our self-worth and self-esteem – if we continually look to others to give that to us – we will always wind up feeling like miserable failures. Why? The answer is that the thoughts, opinions, beliefs, and expectations of others are outside of our control. This mental phenomena constantly fluctuates and changes, meaning that one minute someone may see us as worthy, and the next minute due to a bad mood or something totally frivolous, we may be seen as unworthy. Can you see how unstable our self-worth is when we base it on others opinions? It's like trying to build a house on quicksand: we're always doomed to feel unworthy if we're constantly trying to gain validation from others.

Instead, understand that you are *fundamentally* worthy. You don't need to *do* or *be* anything to be worthy. You are innately, fundamentally, irrevocably worthy. Just look at all parts of nature: none of them would exist if they had no worth. Everything has a purpose, everything has a worth, and so do you. You are part of the ecosystem, part of nature, part of life itself, and that makes you intrinsically worthy and important. Remember that.

20. Learn how to support and comfort yourself

Instead of supporting ourselves when we're hurting inside, we often choose to drown out our pain by indulging in food, sex, social media, relationship drama, and so forth because it feels too overwhelming to face our suffering. These are normal behaviors. However, learning how to face our hurt, instead of escaping from it is one of the most crucial life skills out there. It's also a direct path to self-love.

When we listen to our emotional needs and open ourselves up to the vulnerability of experiencing shame, anger, and grief, we can then take the appropriate steps to help soothe the hurt we feel in a healthy and productive way.

One of the best ways to listen, and open to, our suffering is to connect with the feelings in our bodies. The next time you feel overwhelmed with feelings of anxiety, annoyance, or sadness, ask yourself, "how does this feel in my body?" Give the feeling a color, shape, or texture to make it concrete. Then, gently breathe into that felt experience. Does it transform, expand, shrink, or something else altogether? Hold space for these feelings without trying to force your pain away (this just buries it deeper within you). Using mindfulness, anchor yourself to your five senses and allow the energy to move through you. You might feel the need to hug yourself, jump up and down, punch a pillow, or something else to expel that energy – and if so, give yourself permission.

If you would like to explore how to connect with your body more in order to process emotions and support yourself, research the fields of somatic experiencing and focusing. (See the Bibliography at the end of the book for recommendations.)

I hope these tips and techniques help you to cultivate more self-love in your life. The more love you have for yourself, the easier it will be to retrieve, reintegrate, and heal any lost inner parts and reconnect with your Soul.

In the next chapter, we'll explore the practice of *shadow work*: the final Soul Retrieval path, and the most complex of all. However, by willingly facing our dark side, we remove the blockages that stand in the way of experiencing our Souls once and for all.

"There is no coming to consciousness without pain. People will do anything, no matter how absurd, in order to avoid facing their own soul. One does not become enlightened by imagining figures of light, but by making the darkness conscious."

— **Carl Gustav Jung**

CHAPTER 10

Shadow Work

The final method of Soul Retrieval is something known as Shadow Work; an advanced inner work practice that requires the utmost gentleness and mindfulness.

Our spiritual journey is a bit like the famous story of Dante's Inferno. Before making our way out of our personal "hell," we must walk through the depths (and many layers) of our inner darkness. Many religions explore these experiences well. Two famous examples include the case of Jesus who had to face Satan in the desert and Buddha's encounter with Mara (the Buddhist Satan) before his awakening.

Shadow Work is the practice of exploring this inner darkness. It involves identifying, accepting, loving, and integrating all the parts of yourself that you believe are secretly shameful, embarrassing, unacceptable, ugly, or scary. These secretive and locked-away parts within us form what is known as the *Shadow Self*: the dark side of our nature.

All throughout the history of humankind Shadow Work has played an influential yet mysterious and occult role in helping us discover what is causing us mental illness, physical dis-ease, and even insanity resulting in crimes of all kinds.

Traditionally, Shadow Work fell in the realm of the shamans, or medicine people, as well as the priests and priestesses of the archaic periods of history. These days, Shadow Work falls more commonly in the realms of psychotherapy, with psychologists, psychiatrists, and therapists setting up practices and writing books of all kinds on the topic.

However, more often than not, the prescription drugs and behavioral therapy recommended and appointed to us does little to truly help us make peace with our deepest and darkest thoughts and desires.

The Birth of the Shadow Self

We were all born pure, like blank canvases. But at some point during our childhood development, we learned knowledge that taught us to separate things into good and evil.

Since we were tiny infants we were taught what was "good" and what was "bad," what was "right" and what was "wrong," and what was "virtuous" and what was a plain old "sin." We were punished by our parents when we behaved in a way they didn't like and given love only when we behaved *appropriately.* This taught us that *some* parts of our nature were acceptable, while others weren't (and therefore those parts of us didn't deserve love).

In the context of our larger social conditioning, we were taught that if we stepped out of line in any way, we would either be punished by our parents, the authorities, or by God. Some of us, in our religious education, were even taught that God/Divinity could "hear all of our thoughts," was omnipresent, and would send us to hell for eternity if we were "bad" in any way. This religious and societal brainwashing was enough to make us constantly feel on edge and ridden with guilt. As a result, this pervasive sense of shame and anxiety led to us splitting our nature into "good" and "bad."

In essence, most of us grew up with a 24/7 surveillance system around us. If it wasn't our parents who condemned us, it was our peers, and if it wasn't our peers, it was society, and if it wasn't society, it was a wrathful God. Naturally, this sensationalized the "bad," "evil," and "sinful" acts of life, giving them an all too tempting air of mystery.

To the naturally curious and inquisitive human being, being told that something is "bad" and we "shouldn't do it" is paramount to painting big red words on a wall that say "DON'T PRESS THIS BUTTON!" or "DON'T OPEN THIS DOOR!" Naturally, most of us will push that button and will open that door at some point, giving in to the tempting and sensationalized air of mystery that "evil" and "sinful" acts are given.

But the aftermath is what we suffer from the most.

Once we do taste what it's like to act out in a self-destructive way or have a "bad thought," most of us avoid the shame we feel by repressing it. Eventually, this repression of dark energy builds up within us so much so that, throughout time, we either become physically or psychologically ill (or both). Alternatively, we may decide to act on our dark desires to purge the overwhelmingly tempting curiosity from our systems.

As a result of repressing that which is perceived as "bad" within us, the Shadow Self is born.

The Shadow Self is an accumulation of repressed parts of our nature that resides within the unconscious mind. This "darker half" of our ourselves is composed of all our repressed instincts, impulses, weaknesses, desires, thoughts, and embarrassing fears. This place is often described as the darker side of the psyche, representing wildness, chaos, and the unknown.

Repression of the Shadow Self

It's understandable that the process of becoming civilized requires us to repress aspects of ourselves that do not fit in with the structured ideal of our society. However, it comes at a great cost to us. We are born Whole and complete, but we slowly learn to live fragmented lives, accepting some parts of our nature but rejecting and ignoring other parts.

A holiday to different parts of the world, for example, will show you how arbitrary some of these "good/bad" divisions are (that create the Shadow Self). In the West, for example, eye contact is perceived as confident and engaging, whereas in Japan, it's perceived as arrogant and rude. In the Middle East burping after a meal is a sign of pleasure, yet anywhere else in the world, it's seen as vulgar and uncouth. And in America, TV shows depicting violent murders are considered more acceptable than showing nudity or sexual acts, whereas in Europe it's the complete opposite. These are just a few examples.

Apart from the social and religious role in forming the Shadow Self, modern spirituality has a surprising part to play in Shadow formation as well.

If you notice, a lot of modern spiritual and religious work revolves around moving towards the "light," accepting the light and seeking for the light. Many seekers of spiritual growth think that somehow all of the negative qualities within themselves will eventually be transcended as they "awaken to their Higher Selves," "work through their karma," or "become more enlightened." Yet by avoiding the darkness, they are ignoring what it is to be human! In fact, many spiritual and new age teachings out there provide an escape for those who do not want to be responsible for the entirety of themselves and their lives.

When you take a close look at many spiritual and religious movements, you'll notice that they completely ignore or condemn the darker elements within ourselves such as anger, vengeance, control, fear, shame, competitiveness, jealousy, and lust. Because these darker characteristics are associated with negativity or "evil," they're avoided out of fear and buried even deeper within us. But this is a tragic mistake with dire consequences.

The more our darkness is avoided, the more it grows within us, waiting like a tsunami to gush out at any unexpected moment. The more our darkness is avoided, the more it grows in power because it thrives on fear, secrecy, and shame. The only way out is through. The only way to *ascend* is first to *descend* and meet our Shadows face-to-face.

The Power of Integration

"I must also have a dark side if I am to be whole."

— CARL JUNG

The repression of our negative traits, thoughts, and emotions in society is one of the biggest barriers in any person's journey towards living from the Soul. *How can you completely and wholeheartedly accept who you are if there are sides of yourself that you're too afraid to explore?*

Without facing these thoughts, feelings, traits, and repressed desires within us, we increase the power of our Shadow Selves. And the more powerful our Shadows become, the more likely they are to burst into our waking reality, wreaking havoc and destruction, like a volcano that simply cannot contain its lava any longer.

So how can we face our Shadow Self in a non-destructive, non-condemnatory way? The answer is through *integration* which comes from the Latin word *integratus*, meaning "to make whole."

To integrate an inner Shadow quality is to take ownership and responsibility for it, rather than rejecting or denying it. The benefits are many: sanity, healing, greater compassion, calmness, understanding, and Wholeness are all to be found in integration. This is the essence of Shadow Work.

On the other hand, the opposite of integration is to "*disintegrate*" – or to become fragmented and divided into pieces. A person that "breaks down" or "falls apart," for instance, is someone who is unable to handle stress and who has ignored too many of their personality traits, especially Shadow qualities, to function normally. In reality, a fragmented person can never handle adversity because they have no Whole center: they're always handling life from the corners of their personality parts. This is why integration is so essential: it helps us to become Whole again.

How to Practice Shadow Work

"The secret is out: all of us, no exceptions, have qualities we won't let anyone see, including ourselves – our Shadow. If we face up to our dark side, our life can be energized. If not, there is the devil to pay. This is one of life's most urgent projects."

– LARRY DOSSEY

Shadow Work is primarily a practice of radical self-love, acceptance, and inner integration. When I write about loving or integrating your Shadow Self, I do not mean to indulge in any desire that arises within you. Indulging your anger, for instance, will just result in more anger.

By embracing your inner darkness, I mean that it is necessary for you to "accept" it. Accepting your darkness will allow you to take responsibility for yourself, and once you truly acknowledge your darkness instead of avoiding it, suddenly, it will integrate: it will stop having control over you.

By being honest with ourselves and accepting our Shadow elements, we are free to witness the uncharted areas of our minds. This brutal honesty allows us to see that we are not defined by these dark elements, but instead that we simply possess thoughts, feelings, and drives that come and go. You cannot just go "beyond hatred" if first, you don't admit to yourself that you do, in fact, possess hateful feelings.

To completely experience self-love and reconnect with our Souls, we must learn to voyage into the dark, murky waters of the unknown courageously. We must approach our Shadows with respect, understanding, and compassion – acknowledging both the hidden gifts and curses they offer to us.

A Whole and balanced self is a reconciliation of all parts, an inner unification. It is not an indulgence of the darker parts of our natures, but an acceptance and direct experience of them in the light of mindful awareness and deep honesty. This approach is the entire opposite of many self-denying traditional spiritual methods of subduing, denying, or ascetically disciplining the self.

Thankfully, exploring your darkness is not necessarily all doom and gloom. In fact, you'll likely be surprised by the endless array of creative and interesting things you find that have been secretly buried away for years.

To accept and embrace your Shadow Self is to become Whole again and thus taste a glimpse of what authentic "holiness" feels like.

Here are some simple, but powerful Shadow Work techniques that will help you to integrate your Shadow and reconnect with your Soul again:

1. Art therapy

Art is the highest form of self-expression and also a great way to enable your Shadow to manifest itself. In psychotherapy, an effective way to better understand a client is through art therapy: to allow them to draw whatever they're feeling or thinking. But you don't necessarily need a therapist in order to do this activity.

Simply get a blank piece of paper, find a quiet place, and turn your attention inwards. You may like to ask your Shadow, "*what do you want me to know right now?*" and then paint or draw whatever comes to mind. Even the strangest mental images or scenarios can hold a seed of wisdom, helping to reveal hidden feelings, thoughts, or memories.

Make sure you approach this activity non-judgmentally and with an open mind. When you fear judgment from yourself, you'll be inhibited and won't be able to benefit fully from this practice. So be gentle and receptive. Allow whatever to arise, arise. Remember that your Shadow is a *part* of you, but it doesn't define you.

2. Journal work

Goethe's *Faust* is, in my opinion, one of the best works featuring the meeting of an Ego and his Shadow Self. His story details the life of a professor who becomes so separated and overwhelmed by his Shadow that he comes to the verge of suicide, only to realize that the redemption of the Ego is solely possible if the Shadow is redeemed at the same time.

Writing a story where you project your Shadow elements onto the characters is a great way to learn more about your inner darkness.

If stories aren't your thing, try journaling or keeping a diary every day for a few weeks where you record both good and bad emotions, thoughts, and habits. This practice will help shine a light on the bright and darker elements of your nature. Reading through your journal entries can also help you recover the balance you need in your life, and accept both light and dark emotions within you.

3. Identify sources of projection

Projection is at the very heart and soul of the Shadow: it's how the Shadow hides and protects itself.

Quite simply, *we project the qualities of ourselves that we dislike onto others so that we don't have to deal with them within ourselves.* Projection also helps us to avoid taking responsibility for ourselves and instead helps us to make *others* the culprits and scapegoats for our unresolved issues.

However, projection is actually a powerful Shadow Work tool that helps us explore our Shadow Selves when done deliberately. When you approach other people and the world at large with mindfulness, you'll be able to discover who and what you project your Shadow onto (and why).

What's interesting about the Shadow is that we not only project our negative traits and elements onto others but our good ones as well. It's as if we unconsciously refuse to embrace our noble elements because the ego is afraid that these positive qualities will change and upset our current personality structure.

So how can you practice the projection technique?

In a nutshell, use the world as a mirror. Observe what you secretly like or dislike in other people, entertainment outlets (TV, books), and situations. Observe what elicits a strong emotional reaction from you. Ask yourself, "*What am I feeling right now about this person/situation and what does it say about me?*" and "*What/who is the recipient of my projection?*"

Likely, you will discover patterns frequently emerging in your life. For example, you might be outraged or embarrassed every time sex appears in a TV show or movie you like (possibly revealing sexual repression or mistaken beliefs about sex that you've adopted throughout life). Or you might be terrified of seeing death or dead people (potentially revealing your resistance to the nature of life or a childhood trauma). Or you might be disgusted by alternative political, sexual, and spiritual lifestyles (possibly revealing your hidden desire to believe in or explore these paths). Or you might be outraged by judgmental and narrow-minded people (possibly revealing your own harsh self-judgment).

There are so many possibilities out there, and I encourage you to go slowly, take your time, and one-by-one explore what makes you angry, afraid, seduced, enchanted, or disgusted. You might also like to supplement this activity with journal work and keep a record of what you discover.

Projection is a direct pathway into the Shadow that can be observed in nearly *every* aspect of life – so there are ample opportunities for you to observe your tendency to project in action.

For instance, current movies and television shows reflect our deep interest in the darker aspects of ourselves. Why else would we have such fascination with this constant battle between good and evil forces? Superhero, fantasy, or action films depict the Heroes vs. Villains dichotomy, while we also fall in love with charming characters that embrace their dark sides such as Dexter, The Joker, or Walter White (Breaking Bad).

Furthermore, often, our noblest Shadow traits are projected onto the people we like, admire, or fall in love with. Our disowned qualities such as confidence, passion, sensitivity, creativity, sensuality, and open-mindedness can all be projected onto our beloveds and social idols. The opposite is also true, and the most defenseless of beings can become the carriers of our negative projected Shadow Self traits. Children, for example, provide the perfect outlet for our anger, frustration, and other unsavory qualities such as the obsessive need to control or manipulate. The smallest of accidents or naughty actions can be punished with disproportionate and destructive wrath. Pets too are unfortunately just as vulnerable. Projection, for many of us, is always easier than assimilation and taking self-responsibility.

Ultimately, projection, no matter whether light or dark, is always something detrimental. Not only do you burden another person with your dark elements or pressures of idolization, but you also avoid taking responsibility for your Shadow and lose the opportunity of finding a state of ecstatic Wholeness.

So use the world as your mirror. Write down what you observe about yourself. Be open-minded and receptive. Show kindness toward yourself. Soon you will be on your way to reclaiming all parts of yourself and move closer toward Wholeness.

4. Dream Work

In the West, psychologists believe that dreams are the unconscious mind's way of making sense of reality. But in ancient cultures, such as in Egypt and Greece, dreams were messages from the spirits, gods, or divine realm. Many indigenous cultures have also used dreams as a gateway to higher consciousness and revelation (such as the Native Americans).

These days, most healers agree that dreams express important truths about our lives and destinies. In my experience, dreams can also serve as doorways to our Shadow Selves and true inner feelings.

For this Shadow Work practice, pay attention to your dreams and the images, symbols, and scenarios within them. What stands out to you? What types of recurring feelings, figures, or situations emerge? You might like to keep a dream journal and record your discoveries first thing in the morning.

According to renowned psychologist Carl Jung, the Shadow often appears as characters of the same sex as the dreamer and may appear sinister, repulsive, hostile, ugly, or deformed. It may also come in the form of a ferocious animal, e.g., snake, rabid dog, wild lion – and you may have the sensation of being hunted, chased, threatened, or even attacked by your Shadow. As authors Steve Price and David Haynes note in their book *Dreamworks:*

> *"… shadow elements are some of the most frequently seen dream images … They will usually have a strong, emotional effect on the ego – often a negative one."*

These strong negative feelings are a clear sign that you've had a Shadow dream, so look out for them: they are a direct pathway to meeting your dark side.

More often than not, the message in the dream will be written in the cryptic and symbolic language of the unconscious. Therefore, you'll need to practice unscrambling and deciphering what is being shared with you in order to glean the underlying wisdom.

One of the simplest and most effective ways to find out the deeper meaning of a Shadow dream is to use a basic *free-association* technique. Free-association is essentially the process of spitting out as many thoughts or feelings as you can onto a piece of paper about a topic and making connections between them.

Author Doreen Valiente eloquently describes the practice of free-association:

"A method of interpreting dreams which is often recommended by psychologists, is that of free association. This means that you think over the symbolism of the dream, and record whatever your mind spontaneously associates with it, however irrelevant such an association may at first appear."

Originally created by psychoanalyst Sigmund Freud in the late 1800s, free-association is often used in therapeutic practice to uncover hidden thoughts and feelings that have been repressed. These thoughts and feelings often appear as stories, places, experiences, objects, and sensations within dreams.

But you might be wondering, "How do I go about free-associating by myself?" "Do I need anything in particular?" "Is it difficult?"

The answer is that free-association is just as easy and as simple as making a cup of tea. All you really need is a pen and paper. But to effectively free-associate, you will need to keep a few things in mind:

i) Make sure you have an attitude of non-judgment and curiosity

Free-association is about letting thoughts and words come to you, completely unfiltered. This could mean that you might write down seemingly irrelevant, embarrassing, strange, shocking, or even "crazy sounding" things. Resist the temptation to judge yourself: you will only withhold potentially important and revealing information. The more open you are, the more likely you will understand the meaning of your Shadow dreams.

ii) Write down anything and everything that comes to mind

This is the essence of free-association: spew out anything you think or feel concerning your dream. It's a sort of mental diarrhea. For instance, if you've had a dream about being chased to the edge of a cliff, you might free-associate words such as *"fear of failure, threat, hiding from something, falling, demanding parents, responsibilities, stressed, lost, scared, fed up, walking on eggshells"* and so forth.

iii) Feel free to pause

The difference between free-association and free-writing, is that free-association is done thoughtfully, while free-writing is done as an act of mentally purging all of the thoughts that come into your mind. When you start to free-associate, take time to pause, think, introspect, and dig for a word or feeling – but not for too long (or, not for more than a few seconds)! Free-association is about getting into a gentle flow.

iv) Reflect and draw connections

After you have finished free-associating every word that comes to mind, take a few minutes to reflect on what you have written. What connections can you find? For example, you might have free-associated a dream about traveling to a foreign land with words like *"adventure, change, desire for more, want to do something, excitement, big world, explore."*

Reflecting on these words, you might conclude that you want to expand your world and are finally ready for a change to occur in your life. You might also be tired of your old ways and may desire the adventure of new ways of life.

v) The frequency of a dream greatly impacts its significance

Ideally, free-association should be applied to dreams that frequently emerge each night. The more often a certain type of dream appears in your life, the more likely it is of great significance to you. But also, if a dream pops out of the blue which just happens to stun or confound you, by all means, free-associate!

While it might be easier and more convenient to quickly search for the meaning of your dreams online or in a book, true inner work is about looking inside for the answers and realizing that often the most authentic discoveries actually come from within you.

Remember that your Shadow dreams have unique and highly personal meanings that only you can uncover. So be open, curious, and mindful with this practice. It might take a bit of time to get used to, but it's a powerful way to learn the language of your unconscious mind, connect with your Shadow, and awaken to all sides of your nature.

Shadow Integration Practices

Once you have begun exploring the different parts of your Shadow Self, you must learn how to integrate them. In other words, what do you do after you've discovered a repressed fear, belief, memory, or trauma?

The answer is self-love. In fact, self-love and Shadow Work go hand-in-hand: both support each other, and both are inseparable. Without learning to forgive, accept, love, and nurture yourself completely through your new discoveries, you will fall back into the same old patterns of repression and self-loathing.

Some incredibly effective forms of Shadow integration can include:

- Creating a daily healing ritual for yourself
- Giving yourself space and freedom to grieve
- Practicing mindfulness and non-resistance
- Practicing self-compassion and nurturing
- Creatively expressing your emotions through song, artwork, dance, or writing

There are many other techniques, but these are some of the main Shadow integration paths out there. Finally, always choose a practice that feels the most authentic to you for your unique healing process. If a particular technique just "doesn't fit," feel free to discard of it and try something else of your own liking (or unique creation).

Shadow Work is a powerful form of soul retrieval that empowers you on your spiritual awakening journey. To genuinely become a Whole and healed person, you must integrate your Shadow into your being. In other words, you must strive to 100% own your Shadow, rather than avoiding or repressing it.

Remember that what you internalize is almost always externalized in one form or another.

Own your Shadow, and you will own your life.

In the next chapter, we'll explore the many traps and pitfalls spiritual seekers undergo on the path of spiritual awakening. It's crucial that you become aware of these dangers and drawbacks so that you can experience the joy, love, and freedom contained within your Soul.

"Sometimes the route we think is the 'high road' is actually a shortcut called avoidance."

— Randi Buckley

CHAPTER 11

Spiritual Bypassing Traps

There is one significant pitfall that we are all at risk of experiencing on our spiritual awakening journey.

This pitfall is essentially our tendency to ignore the entirety of what it means to be a human being. In other words, it can be very easy for us to ignore the darker elements of who we are, and instead focus on emphasizing our lighter, more comfortable elements of "awakening." This pitfall is known as *spiritual bypassing*.

When we ignore many of the deep-seated and uncomfortable aspects of ourselves, we do ourselves a tremendous disservice.

While it is noble for us to want to search for the good within everything, and while it is virtuous for us to want to use "love" to solve all of humanity's problems, we often fail to acknowledge that we must first overcome the issues we face. These issues include the many erroneous beliefs, psychological traumas, and neglected inner parts that we've failed to heal. Only after we honestly assess ourselves can we allow love and light to be our guiding forces.

For the next part of your journey, it is important that you're aware of the many spiritual bypassing traps out there that can easily ensnare you on your path. Without being conscious of these traps, it is easy for you to get sidetracked, confused, and lost – sometimes for many years on the spiritual awakening path.

Firstly, let's explore the meaning of spiritual bypassing.

What is Spiritual Bypassing?

The term 'spiritual bypassing' was originally coined by psychologist John Welwood in 1984. As he explained in an interview:

"Spiritual bypassing is a term I coined to describe a process I saw happening in the Buddhist community I was in, and also in myself. Although most of us were sincerely trying to work on ourselves, I noticed a widespread tendency to use spiritual ideas and practices to sidestep or avoid facing unresolved emotional issues, psychological wounds, and unfinished developmental tasks."

As we can see, spiritual bypassing is largely about avoiding or escaping from difficult life experiences (and it's not exclusively a Buddhist issue, either). In other words, to spiritually bypass is to use spirituality to avoid, suppress, or escape from uncomfortable issues in life.

These issues could be the loss of a loved one, a relationship breakup, family problems, childhood abuse, loneliness, low self-esteem, self-sabotaging behaviors, fear, mental or emotional health issues, or any other problems life presents.

To many people, spirituality becomes a sort of crutch used as a way of standing back up again in the face of life's turmoil – and sometimes this is necessary. We all need support at some time or another in our lives. But the problem comes when spirituality is used as a drug for which we become dependent on to bypass the darker elements of our lives.

As psychotherapist P. T. Mistlberger writes,

"Many 'feel-good' approaches to personal transformation, or diluted new age teachings, in their rushed desire to reach an idealized state of unity with existence, gloss over the need to face and assume responsibility for one's inner shadow element, or darker nature."

When spirituality is used as a defense mechanism to ward off the gremlins and dirty devils of our lives, it actually becomes our greatest hindrance, preventing us from developing true courage, authenticity, and Wholeness; qualities that refine our Souls. While the use of spirituality can provide us with a solid wall to hide behind, in doing so, it traps us in an all-is-happy-and-perfect jail cell of illusions.

Types of Spiritual Bypassing

"What gives light must endure burning."

— VIKTOR FRANKL

The reality is that not everything in life is "love and light," as is the slogan for many spiritual seekers. Pursuing the light and living an enlightened, raw, and deeply interconnected existence is also about setting yourself on fire. It is about creating an inferno of your false beliefs, illusions, and divisive desires, ideals, and prejudices. It is about surrendering to the destruction of every limiting thing you ever thought and felt about yourself, other people, and the world.

Spirituality is not always pretty. In fact, often it is the most shattering, tumultuous, and testing experience we can go through in life. But only once we emerge from the embers of our destruction can we can be reborn – like phoenixes – into new lives of clarity and purity. The truth is that there are many types of spiritual bypassing that we sometimes don't recognize (or refuse to recognize) in life. I have listed a few examples below that are vital to be aware of on your spiritual awakening path:

1) The Optimistic Bypass

We've all come across people in life who love to laugh and smile, yet seem to be forcefully optimistic. "Focus on the positive!" "See the glass as half full!" "Don't let a frown get you down!" are some of the catchcries of these people who tend to use optimism as a way of avoiding the more somber and troublesome realities of life. The optimistic bypass is often a side product of anger-phobia, or the inability to deal with negative emotions.

2) The Aggrandizement Bypass

This is a type of self-delusion that some spiritual seekers use as a way of masking their perceived deficiencies and insecurities. The aggrandizement bypass is adopted by those who seek to feel like they're enlightened, superior or have reached higher planes of existence. This form of spiritual bypassing is sometimes used by self-proclaimed masters, leaders, awakened souls, and gurus.

3) The Victim Bypass

When one becomes a victim of their gifts (or other people), this takes away the pressure and responsibility for shaping a satisfying life and taking responsibility for one's happiness. This is the biggest issue with the Victim Bypass. Unfortunately, this form of spiritual bypassing is often used by spiritual seekers who believe they have extrasensory gifts of some kind – but due to their gifts, they are unable to feel happy or healthy. While understanding ourselves through labels is helpful (such as 'empath,' 'old soul,' etc.) sometimes the label can be used to reject and condemn others and reinforce our self-destructive behavior.

4) The Psychonaut Bypass

Many spiritual seekers explore the frontiers of the mind, Soul, and reality through the use of psychedelic drugs such as LSD, DMT, psilocybin mushrooms, mescaline, and other entheogens. While this is a fascinating way of exploring reality, entheogens, like any other drug, can sometimes be used as a way of escaping reality and avoiding committing to the hard work of personal development and Soul-centered growth.

5) The Horoscope Bypass

Often, asking for and seeking help from outside sources is crucial for our well-being and spiritual development. But when we *habitually* look outside of ourselves for help and guidance, as is with the case with horoscopes and psychics, we are failing to tap into our inner wellsprings of wisdom and strength and are allowing external predictions to control the outcome of our lives. The Horoscope Bypass is derived from fear and mistrust of ourselves, our inability to make decisions, and our inability to deal with anything tough that comes our way.

6) The Saint Bypass

Most of us have been conditioned to see "spiritual people" as completely kind, compassionate, saint-like, and even otherworldly beings. The Saint Bypass is a reflection of this extreme "black or white" thinking, promoting the underlying belief that spiritual people can't have dark sides because that would make them "unspiritual." Therefore, when many seekers enter the spiritual path, they believe they must match this ideal. Unfortunately, this type of bypassing is essentially an avoidance of one's own Shadow Self by overcompensating with the guise of a sweet, heavenly exterior. Self-sacrifice is a major symptom of this type of bypass, and the result is a pervasive sense of guilt, shame, and "never being good enough."

7) The Spirit Guide Bypass

In some spiritual traditions, it is a God who protects us, in others, it is an angel, animal, or an ascended being. No matter who the Spirit Guide is, the belief that they are there to "protect" us is pleasing to the mind, but restricting to the Soul. When we place our faith in another being's power to ward off danger and keep us safe, we are committing a classic spiritual bypass: avoiding responsibility for ourselves and our lives and sidestepping the tough development of courage and resilience. We are not children, but when we think of ourselves as being so, we mold our lives in such a way that we fail to develop strength of spiritual character. Spirit guides serve to teach us rather than to babysit us.

8) The Praying Bypass

Similar to the Spirit Guide Bypass, the Praying Bypass circumvents personal responsibility by putting faith in a higher being to solve all of our problems and issues. While praying can be a healthy practice, it can easily become limiting if we become too dependent on it.

9) The Guru Bypass

Often it is beneficial to latch onto a particular guru, shaman, or spiritual teacher to learn and grow. However, too much attachment can serve as another form of spiritual bypassing. When we begin to worship another living being, we fall in love with the rose-colored illusory image we have of the teacher rather than the essence of their teachings. Not thinking or discovering truth for ourselves by treating the words of a guru or master as scripture subtracts from our growth and our own self-mastery on our personal spiritual journeys.

10) The Finger-Pointing Bypass

On our spiritual quests, we begin to see through the lies, delusions, and crazy behaviors committed by our fellow human beings, and this can make us angry, downhearted, and greatly frustrated. However, when we get caught up in "everything that is wrong" with the outside world and other people, dedicating our lives to the self-righteous quest of finger-pointing, this can be another form of spiritual bypassing. Finger-pointing instills us with a false sense of righteousness, taking away our responsibility of looking inside and working on ourselves. At its roots, the Finger-Pointing bypass is sourced from fear and avoidance and is a powerful form of procrastination. Yes, sometimes it is necessary to point out what's wrong with others, but when that's *all* we do, we are avoiding facing our own flaws and misguided behavior.

Indeed, there are many other forms of spiritual bypassing, but here I present the most common ones that are easily observable in everyday life. From my own experience, I know how terrifying and embarrassing it can be to expose yourself and your vulnerable parts to the process of spiritual purification – a vital part of the spiritual awakening process. But slowly as you set fire to all illusions and falsities, you see that life is much clearer, more connected, deeply satisfying, and indescribably joyful.

Common Pitfalls on the Path of Awakening

As we've just seen, an enormous obstacle on our journeys of Inner Work and spiritual Wholeness is our tendency to become enamored by the promise of "peace" and "love," and in the process, shy away from experiencing the more challenging and darker elements of self-exploration.

It's not that love and light don't have their places in our journeys — they most certainly do. But if these brighter, more appealing qualities are emphasized to the degree that involves the repression of darkness, and resistance to the harder aspects of inner exploration, then we are creating an imbalance within ourselves.

Often the reason why we embark on a spiritual path in the first place is that we have experienced immense struggles and pain in the past (that are manifested as a spiritual awakening), and have observed the struggles of others around us hopelessly. This suffering tends to awaken a thirst within us to find fulfilling answers that solve why all of these things happen. However, ignoring these "heavier" elements of life in exchange for the "lighter" elements is not a wise approach.

The truth is that when we think about Soul embodiment and spiritual Wholeness, we tend to perceive these experiences as immediately *transcending* and miraculously going *beyond* who we are right now, rather than representing the fulfillment of our inner potentials.

Let me illustrate what I mean by the fulfillment of our potential:

Imagine the transformation of a caterpillar into a butterfly. The caterpillar does not transform into a cocoon and go beyond being a caterpillar. The caterpillar is still a caterpillar inside the cocoon, and it is still a caterpillar once it evolves into a butterfly — only, apart from being a fully actualized caterpillar, it has now grown wings.

The nature of transformation is not to ignore aspects of our nature and fool ourselves into thinking that we have overcome these elements. *Transformation is a process of transcending what was before by integrating it entirely* (or combining all parts within us to make a whole). In doing so, something new within us can blossom.

There are many mistakes that we can make on our journeys of spiritual awakening. Here are the main ones to be conscious of:

1. Trying to lose your ego/self

Many people talk about going "beyond the ego," losing it, and portray it as something evil. The reality is that our sense of self is essential for the development of our individuality and is not innately "bad." Our ego is necessary for our survival as it causes us to see that we are physically separate from others, and therefore we must care for ourselves.

By trying to lose our egos, or by thinking of them as solely "illusions," we run the risk of developing a profound sense of futility with life, a pointlessness in doing anything or relating to anyone. For example, this feeling of futility can be reflected in the belief that "I don't exist so what's the point of doing anything?" or "Others don't exist either, so why bother 'forgiving' or cultivating deep relationships with them?"

It is necessary to realize that transcending your ego first implies developing a healthy and functional ego that operates in the world harmoniously. As transpersonal therapist, P. T. Mistlberger explains:

"The ego is fundamental to individual development and is not inherently bad. It is necessary for both survival and individuation (recognizing who we are in distinction to others) ... we cannot begin to go 'beyond' the ego if we have not first developed it into a functionally health process of relating to the world."

To create a strong ego, we first need to develop inner Wholeness by healing our core wounds and retrieving our Soul parts. Our egos will always be there, but the difference is that when they are healthy and when we are aware of their existence, we stop listening to them and blindly allowing them to influence our decisions or actions.

2. Always being "positive"

Cultivating the habit of positive thinking makes a great difference to many people, especially if they are prone to habitually making negative judgments.

While developing the ability to see the "silver lining" of life can be very beneficial, the very nature of developing a positive attitude involves a constant judgment of the world. In other words, forcing a positive attitude means making constant judgments that separate the world, people, and situations into "good" and "bad." This division of the world leads to attacking anything that is perceived as negative with the belief that thinking positively will make it less bad. This type of thinking can sometimes be harmful as we don't always succeed in our positive expectations, and consequently, we can end up feeling devastated that we failed in changing the outcome.

When we stop judging the world as black and white, when we stop labeling things that happen to us as "good" and "bad," we stop resisting life. We also become less stressed, and there is no necessity to impose a positive outlook on everything forcefully.

3. Trying to become like a child

It is often said that we must return to the state of being a "child" to experience Divinity or Oneness, just as we experienced before we developed a sense of self that created separation between us and existence.

The unity with life that a child experiences is not the same as the unity experienced by an adult. The child experiences a state of "fusion" with life as they haven't yet developed a separate identity and consequently have never tasted anything else. However, the adult who has developed, integrated, and transcended their sense of self, acquires an entirely different experience of unity and deep connection with life. This unity experienced by the adult is one of responsibility and of awareness of the interconnectedness between themselves and existence.

This sense of responsibility is what determines whether we regress to a *"childish"* state where we shift our personal responsibility onto outside forces (like God or Karma), or whether we develop a *"childlike"* being that is entirely aware of the effects of our actions due to our feeling of unity with life.

4. Believing that logic and rationality are "evil"

As we progress through our paths of spiritual awakening, we begin to experience moments of complete inner silence, deep peace, inner revelations, and insights into our unity with existence beyond our individual sense of self. It is through these experiences that we start transcending the mind.

When we undergo these mystical moments, we have no thoughts, we feel infinitely expansive, and we tap into our True Nature. However, sometimes through these experiences, we tend to start thinking that logic and rationality are "evil" or are "bad" parts of ourselves that prevent us from experiencing these profound states more. And so we begin to associate all kinds of non-rational states with "spiritual experiences."

Our minds are tools, which, when not mastered, can lead us astray and can cause us immense amounts of suffering. But the vital thing to remember is that the mind itself isn't at fault; *we* are at fault for allowing it to control us in such extreme ways. It is our logic and rationality, for example, that stops us from jumping in front of oncoming traffic because we feel "One" with the truck.

Let your passion and intuition be the sails of your ship, but allow reason to be the rudder that guides you.

5. Only focusing on higher chakras

Hinduism teaches the idea that we all possess seven different bodily energy centers that we can access called *chakras*. In fact, this notion of energy centers being present within the human body is found in many different cultures in some form or another (for example, in Peru we call them "*Chunpis*," or "Belts" of power which extend around our bodies).

Many teachings that use chakra centers for their work encourage you to focus on your "higher" centers such as the "Crown," "Head," and "Heart" chakras while ignoring the lower ones such as the Solar Plexus, Sacral, and Root Chakras. For many people who require a lot of harmonizing done in their lower centers, this does not lead to a balanced being.

Let me give you an illustration that might explain what I mean better:

Imagine a very tall building where the first few floors are ignored completely and are rarely maintained, while the top floors are glorified, swept, mended, and polished daily. The reality is that it doesn't matter how beautiful the top of the building is if the lower floors are not given the attention they need: the whole building will crumble to the ground as the lower floors form the very foundation of the entire structure. The same goes with the work we apply to the chakras.

When we deny the lower chakras, we deny the totality of our being, which is unhealthy, short-sighted, and detrimental to our spiritual growth.

6. Ignoring your darkness

As mentioned in the previous chapter, we all naturally form a self-image or ego that we present to other people. In doing so, we simultaneously create a "Shadow Self," which is primarily composed of the elements that we want to prevent other people and ourselves from seeing. Therefore, we unconsciously repress many aspects of ourselves that we perceive as "bad" or "dirty." Such traits include, for example, our sexuality, our fears, our vulnerabilities, our secret desires, our "immoral" thoughts, and so forth. When we reject these various elements of ourselves, we create a "dual nature" within us.

Our Shadow Selves usually only manifest themselves under certain types of pressure that prevent us from containing them anymore. Examples include when we are under great stress, experience intense emotions like anxiety, in an altered state of consciousness (such as through drug use), or any other experience that brings down our guard.

These disowned parts of ourselves can influence a lot of our behavior, and drain a tremendous amount of our energy. Our Shadow Selves, or our personal "demons," gain even more power when we are taught through cultural and quasi-spiritual teachings to focus solely on getting in touch with, and manifesting, our "inner gods" and "goddesses" and the light side of our being.

This chronic tendency to avoid our inner darkness is why it's important for you to revise the chapter of Shadow Work in this book!

True Inner Healing

To become Whole and healed beings, we must walk the path of the middle: we must experience both the light and dark, "good" and "bad," and beautiful and horrific parts of ourselves. The only way to truly and authentically progress on your journey of spiritual awakening is to experience and integrate, as much of your nature as possible.

By becoming aware of these spiritual traps and pitfalls, you will arm yourself with knowledge, clarity, and awareness. While the truth can hurt, it's essential that you're honest with yourself and regularly examine where you may be lost or stuck in a pattern of spiritual bypassing. In doing so, you will liberate yourself and remove the inner barriers that hold you back from experiencing your True Nature.

In the final chapter, we'll explore how to finally connect with the core of your being: your Soul. After all the complex inner work we've just explored in the previous chapters, you'll be relieved to discover that connecting with your Soul is a simple, refreshing, and wondrous practice.

"Through our soul is our contact with heaven."

— Sholem Asch

CHAPTER 12

Soul Communication

Once you have explored the sources of your Soul Loss, and undergone the many practices associated with Soul Retrieval (including being conscious of the many spiritual traps out there), contacting your Soul becomes a simple and joyful experience.

The entire purpose of the spiritual awakening process is to learn how to retrieve, heal, but also communicate with your Soul. We refer to this as *Soul communication*.

Soul communication is such a vital skill to develop because it can help you discover not only your life purpose but also many of your innate spiritual gifts and talents. Soul communication also opens the sacred doorway into experiencing complete Wholeness, Enlightenment, and Union with the Divine.

Contacting the Soul

Every day, our Soul speaks to us in a thousand different ways. However, shamans, medicine people, mystics, and sages throughout the ages have always known that the Soul doesn't speak the human language.

Instead, *our Soul communicates with us through symbols, metaphors, archetypes, poetry, deep feelings, and magic.* The human language is far too limiting to express the full spectrum of profound knowledge, insight, and revelation that the Soul has to share.

As such, most of us were never taught to tune into the dancing rhythms of our deepest selves. Instead, due to our social conditioning, we have come to rely heavily on the mind and its interpretation of reality. Unfortunately, our emphasis on hard data, facts, and linear logic has left a gaping hole inside of us. We fill this empty hole with consumerism, addictions, violence, and endless distractions – but none of it genuinely satiates our deep spiritual impoverishment.

Sometimes, a traumatic or extreme event in our lives shakes us out of our habitual way of perceiving existence. But usually, most of us tend to miss the big, glaring daily signs that the Soul within us is trying to communicate with us. Not only that, but we tend to actively mistrust, ignore, or doubt any sacred form of communication that we receive denouncing it as "delusional" or "irrelevant."

How can we begin to tune into the subtle voice of the Soul and rewire our conditioned brains? How can we listen to our Soul's vital messages and nourish ourselves with its life-changing, heart-opening wisdom?

Signs to Look Out For

Soul communication isn't just reserved for medicine men or women or enlightened people; it is a birthright of every man, woman, and child.

For years both of us lived without the guidance of our Souls, actively ignoring and numbing them out. Since reconnecting with our Souls, we've discovered that they offer endless gifts, insights, teachings, and direction that help us to connect with our innate Wholeness, and guide others to do the same.

If you'd like to learn Soul communication, you must first pay attention to the signs that your Soul is subtly sending you. While there are many types of signs out there, we have compiled some of the main ones below that you should look out for:

1. Dream signs

Our Souls communicate with us through images, symbols, and scenarios in our dreamscapes. In fact, our dreams can be thought of as portals into the unconscious mind. Your unconscious mind is a bridge to the Soul and an unlimited source of wisdom. So pay close attention to your dreams. What metaphorical or literal message is being conveyed to you each night? What objects, people, sounds, or words stand out and call your attention? Keep a dream journal and use the free-association technique we outlined in chapter 10 to decode the meaning of your dreams. Soul-based dreams are often exceptionally vivid, meaningful, otherworldly, inspiring, and even healing on an indescribable level.

2. Lucid dreams

Spontaneous lucid dreams involve suddenly becoming aware that you're dreaming while being asleep. Becoming conscious within your dream world is not only spiritually symbolic (literally of "waking up"), but it is also an opportunity to explore the hidden realm of your unconscious mind. This opportunity from your Soul might be rare, or it could be constant without any effort on your behalf.

If you're in the habit of having spontaneous lucid dreams, treat it as a sacred gift. Very few people have access to the depths of the unconscious realms. Treat this as an opportunity to ask yourself questions and find guidance that you wouldn't be able to otherwise access in waking life.

On the other hand, you might like to look into the practice of learning how to lucid dream and using that as a gateway to direct Soul communication.

3. Repetitive words or numbers

How many times have you looked at the clock and seen "11:11," "12:12," "13:13," "4:44"? Many skeptics say that putting importance into repetitive words and numbers is a reflection of something called "confirmation bias" (or the tendency to interpret events in favor of your beliefs), but this is not necessarily the case. It's easy to be cynical and use a purely logical approach, but it's much harder to explore the personal meaning of these experiences and dig deep.

Regardless of the meaning we assign to repetitive words and numbers, the function of them is to momentarily "wake us up." Otherwise, why would we give them so much significance? Whenever I see a repeated number or hear a name/word said continuously, I take it as a sign of Soul communication. There's a reason why it constantly catches your attention, and that's because it has *personal significance* to you.

So whenever you hear or see a picture, word, or number repeated, ask yourself, *what is the hidden message here?* Repetitive words or numbers are like sacred breadcrumbs scattered throughout your day, leading you on the path to a greater level of understanding and awakening.

4. Animal omens and guides

Most of us come across animals every day. Quite often, unbeknownst to us, these animals serve as omens and guides that symbolize warnings or different types of wisdom. When you pay attention to the various animals you see each day, you'll realize that each one has a specific teaching, message, or energy type.

It's important to keep in mind that the meaning you assign to the different animals you see is highly personal and not necessarily the "orthodox" meaning already established out there. So don't feel the need to go by the textbook definition. Go with your gut.

One way of discovering your unique Soul messages is to observe what animals you consistently come across every day. Watch these animals and try to understand what their teachings are. What are they revealing? How do they behave, move, or sound? Paying attention to the animals that appear to you throughout your days is an important form of Soul communication.

For example, you might continually come across crows. Watching these crows, you might realize that they are always loud and agitated. The message you might discover from these animal messengers is that you need to pay more attention to the emotions you have suppressed so that they can be released. Another example is frequently seeing spiders everywhere, often in the most bizarre places (like on your laptop or in your car). You might discover that a pattern keeps emerging: every time you feel depressed, you keep seeing spiders. Upon reflection, you might realize that this animal messenger is teaching you about the interconnectedness of life (the spider weaves webs that are symbolic of connectedness) and that you're not alone.

5. Synchronicity or serendipity

Have you ever had a string of events happen in a way that seemed unique or out of the ordinary? You might refer to these events as "serendipity" when in fact they may have been more accurately known as "*synchronicity*."

What is synchronicity? Synchronicities are moments of meaningful coincidence, where our inner and outer worlds align. Often synchronicity is an excellent way to tell that you are on the right Soul path because everything feels *right* and as though life is unfolding without your conscious effort. You might even have the sensation that Life/Spirit/God is playing an active hand in making your dreams or aspirations come true.

For example, you might want to quit your job to follow your dreams as a therapist. Throughout the next few days, you may have vivid dreams of helping to counsel people. Then, at work, you receive the news that you're getting a pay cut. After that, you see numerous bumper stickers on cars that say "Natural Therapy Association Member." Shortly after, you may keep overhearing people mentioning the word "therapy" in their conversations. Finally, you discover an advert in the local newspaper for a therapist course being held in your area. This scenario is one example of a string of synchronicity.

Science attests to the fact that everything is energy, and is thus connected. Therefore, it's my belief that nothing happens by chance, and coincidence is an illusion. At a core Soul and Spirit level, *everything is interconnected.* So what is synchronicity? In my understanding, it is when the vibration of our thoughts matches the vibration of our personal destinies. In other words, picture synchronicity like a funnel of water: you don't need to force the water to go through, the water goes through effortlessly.

So watch out for moments of synchronicity — they are powerful reflections that you're on the right path, and Life is helping you to actualize your destiny.

6. Gut feelings

A gut feeling is an unexplainable sensation that tells you to do (or not do) something. Another synonym for this phrase is the word *intuition* – also known as the voice of your Soul. Whenever you feel drawn towards something or someone (without a fearful motive), you can be sure that this is your Soul trying to guide you. This is why listening to, and sharpening, your intuition is a powerful way of maintaining contact with your Soul.

While we all know what intuition is, unfortunately, most of us have trouble listening to it due to the voice of fear within our minds. So how can we distinguish the two? Intuition is different from the inner voice of fear because it is subtle, calm, and centered, as opposed to being frantic, anxiety-fuelled, or aggressive. This distinction is crucial to make. Many people believe they are being guided by intuition when, in fact, they are being guided by their fearful inner talk. So remember this: *intuition is clear and calm while the voice of fear is vague and irritable.* When you learn how to make this distinction, listening to your intuition will become an effortless process.

Listening to your intuition is also a key way to pay attention to Soul signs. For instance, you might feel a little nudge (that has no logical explanation) to go to a certain place at a certain time. As a result of listening to this little nudge, you might run into a long lost friend or future soul mate who may positively change your life forever. Or you might be pulled toward a specific line of work that embodies your true life purpose. Look out for these subtle nudges, pulls, tugs, and whispers and learn to track them.

7. Visions during meditation

Meditation is another way to receive messages from, and contact, your Soul. If you've ever meditated before, you may have had the privilege of entering that calm, wise, clear, and infinitely loving place within you which I call your *Soul space.*

Meditating for extended periods (30 minutes or more) is a powerful way to experience your Soul space – which is sometimes referred to as having a *mystical experience*. One common mystical experience people have during meditation involves tuning into visions or spontaneous names. These visions or names are often direct messages from your Soul. I've even had people tell me that they've received unknown songs or melodies during meditation – sometimes in totally foreign languages. Personally, I have experienced spontaneous visions and words during meditation that have helped me to learn a great deal about myself and tap into higher levels of consciousness.

But how can you tell normal mental chatter apart from Soulful visions, names, or songs? Typically, the images you see or words you hear will have a particular theme that seems foreign (e.g., it could be from an ancient culture such as an African tribe), and the images, sounds, or melodies will be very repetitive, yet gentle. You will also have the sensation that you somehow need to pay attention to these spontaneous occurrences and that they're important, even sacred.

I recommend keeping a meditation journal to record these visions, images, words, or songs. Maintaining a journal will help you to articulate better what your Soul is trying to express and inspire you to keep going deep within yourself.

How to Speak to Your Soul

There are many ways for you to communicate actively with your Soul. *Art, journaling, dancing, singing, and contemplation* are all profound ways of communing with this core part of you.

However, there are some practices that are universally applicable and easy to incorporate into your life. I'll elaborate on these five paths below:

Practice 1 – Make friends with solitude

Solitude will be your greatest ally when it comes to connecting with your Soul. How else can you listen to the whispers and catch the wisps of your Soul in a chaotic, noisy world? The answer is that it's extremely difficult unless you have undergone years of rigorous meditation training or have attained a rare awakened state of being.

To make friends with solitude, you'll need to set aside a regular time and space to spend with yourself away from others. Disconnect from technology, unplug (or turn off) the phone, and find a quiet place undisturbed from other people. Most people benefit the most from solitude when it's a regular, consistent, and daily practice. Think about dedicating ten minutes to half an hour (or ideally more) to spending time with yourself.

What you choose to do within this time is entirely up to you, but I recommend keeping it simple. Most of your energy, after all, needs to be directed inwards. Examples of solitary spiritual activities you could try include mindfully making a cup of tea, walking outside in the sunlight, focusing on your breathing, listening to silence, watching a candle flame, strolling through the woods, and so on. Choose a simple activity that calls to you. And remember, the mundane can be sacred too. Even folding the clothes and doing the laundry can be sacred if done with a quiet, contemplative heart.

In these still, silent, meditative moments, you will be able to speak to or dwell directly in, your Soul. So treat this practice like watching a deer in the forest: the utmost gentleness, quietness, and stillness is required to let the ego fade and the Soul shine.

Practice 2 – Connect with nature and the wildness within you

Nature is tremendously healing and revivifying to the human Soul. It is the perfect medium through which we can feel, experience, and communicate with our deeper Being.

Sadly, most of us carry the unspoken belief that we're separate from nature: we're human and "above" nature, after all, right? Wrong. We're an inseparable part of nature. Our blood, bones, hair, skin, and entrails are all the stuff of the earth: animalistic, carnal, corporeal.

As psychologist John Welwood writes:

The human spirit, despite centuries of superficial domestication, retains a fundamentally wild quality. It is wild in the way that wind, rain, and sun are, wild in this sense meaning "untampered with; as it is, in itself." This elemental wildness is not something crude or primitive. It is, rather, a reality beyond personality or conditioning: the god or goddess living and moving deep within, whose power nourishes us like a clear, pristine underground spring.

To get in touch with our basic wildness is to unite with a fundamental quality of the Soul: freedom. And the best way to tap into this inner wildness can be found in the bosom of Mother Nature.

It's not difficult or taxing to reconnect with nature. All it requires is just a couple of minutes a day outside, mindfully observing the trees, the animals, the clouds, and the sun rays beaming through the clouds. If you're lucky enough to live close to a natural reserve, you might like to practice the Japanese art of Forest Bathing or take a blanket and have a picnic. If you're in the city, there's still the opportunity to connect with nature. Go to the local park, listen to various sounds of nature on your phone, buy a potted plant. When your heart is open, there are endless ways for nature to creep, dig, weave, and sprout its way into your life.

Practice 3 – Find your soul space and place

Sound confusing? Let me differentiate the two:

A *Soul place* is a physical location that deeply calls to you: it speaks to your Soul. You might feel a sense of nostalgic longing for this place, a sense of deep resonance, and almost mystical significance.

Soul places can be mundane areas (such as your backyard), untouched areas (such as a place in the wilderness), or holy sites (such as Stonehenge, Uluru, Notre Dame Cathedral, etc.). You will feel a sense of expansion in these places, deep peace, and like you have finally 'found home.' *What has happened is that you've found an external representation of the inner heaven within you.* That's why Soul places touch us so profoundly.

Your *Soul space*, on the other hand, is an inner experience of your True Nature. We often inhabit our Soul spaces in moments of prayer, contemplation, altered states of consciousness, and deep meditation.

As poet and spiritual writer Mark Nepo writes:

Each person is born with an unencumbered spot—free of expectation and regret, free of ambition and embarrassment, free of fear and worry—an umbilical spot of grace where we were each first touched by God. It is this spot of grace that issues peace. Psychologists call this spot the Psyche, theologians call it the Soul, Jung calls it the Seat of the Unconscious, Hindu masters call it Atman, Buddhists call it Dharma, Rilke calls it Inwardness, Sufis call it Qalb, and Jesus calls it the Center of our Love. To know this spot of Inwardness is to know who we are, not by surface markers of identity, not by where we work or what we wear or how we like to be addressed, but by feeling our place in relation to the Infinite and by inhabiting it.

To inhabit this Soul space, we need to break through the barriers of the ego through various methods of inner work (such as self-love, inner child work, and shadow work) – that is the *doing* side of things. The other side is *being*: we need a practice that helps us to cultivate inner stillness and silence. And the best method I know of for experiencing this state is meditation. Generally, any meditation technique will do. But I have personally found Vipassana and Mindfulness Meditation to be the two meditation methods that have worked the most profoundly for me. (I recommend that you explore these practices further and also discover your own preferred meditation method.)

By combining both inner work techniques and meditation, we balance all levels of our being and increasingly embody our True Nature. And finally, as Turkish poet and Sufi mystic Yunus Emre writes, we discover that:

"I am the drop that contains the sea. How beautiful to be an ocean hidden within an infinite drop."

Practice 4 – Open the sacred doorway of your heart

As human beings having a spiritual experience, we have legs and feet that are connected to the earth and heads that reach the heavens. Unlike most creatures on the planet, we are upright, standing beings: our connection to the earth is symbolic of our animal nature while our connection to the sky is symbolic of our spiritual nature. But at the very center and core of our being, joining these two extremes is the heart.

As a bridge between higher and lower worlds, *the heart is the doorway to the Soul.* It is through the heart that we connect with others, grow, expand, and taste all aspects of existence. It is through the heart that we experience balance, Wholeness, compassion, joy, and freedom: and these are all qualities innate to the Soul.

To communicate with, and gradually become One with your True Nature, your Soul, you must develop a deep, ongoing relationship with your heart. When we stay stranded in earthly issues or get lost in intellectual or cosmic musings, we are disconnected from the very core of our being. The goal here is not to abandon our animal or spiritual nature, the goal is to become more *spiritually embodied:* both human *and* divine. And connecting with the heart is the best way to do that.

Luckily, connecting with the heart is a beautifully simple practice. In essence, all you need to do is *find a way to experience your emotions more fully in the present moment.* Some wonderful examples of this include practicing gratitude, noticing and seeking out beauty, listening to soul-stirring music, journaling about your feelings, showing kindness toward someone, practicing self-compassion, using mindfulness to feel emotions in the present moment, volunteering, opening up to trusted people, hugging, kissing, laughing, dancing, and celebrating life in whatever way you know how. The possibilities are endless, but I have given you a few simple places to start. Listen to your instincts, and go with whatever touches you most deeply. From there, all you need to do is make a practice and habit out of heartfulness (i.e., the art of being in-tune with your heart).

Practice 5 – Embrace the power of prayer

Perhaps the easiest and most powerful method of communing with your Soul is simply to say a daily prayer.

Here is an example you could use, or build on yourself:

"Dear Soul, I love you. Thank you for supporting my life. I'm so honored and appreciative of your presence. If you have any messages for me, please communicate them to me. I am open and receptive. I welcome your guidance."

See how you go with this prayer and ensure that you pay attention to any emotional, physical, or mental sensations that arise. You might like to record whatever you find in a specially dedicated journal.

I hope that you're now more aware of the deep craving of your Soul to make itself known to you. Deep down, we all crave for Oneness and Wholeness. By learning the language of your Soul, and by communing with this sacred Center of your being, you can open a doorway into the world of reclaimed strength, beauty, love, peace, and freedom.

*"Your own Self-Realization
is the greatest service
you can render the world."*

— Ramana Maharshi

Conclusion

There is no personal growth, no awakening in life, and no awakening to life, without first seeing and acknowledging our existing dissatisfaction. This dissatisfaction is not the usual day-to-day kind but is rather a deep, internal disappointment. It is the gaping inner void we all possess which constantly reminds us that something is missing from our lives, and also that something at a core level is lost. Usually, the very thing that is lost is a connection to our Souls.

Although this period of unhappiness, confusion, and longing may feel like a bad thing at first, it is the greatest blessing you could receive. While the spiritual awakening process may seem like a harrowing experience, it's sole purpose is to initiate you into your spiritual journey. Your spiritual journey is the very path that leads you to total peace, liberation, and the discovery that your Soul was, and has always been, perfectly Whole. It is only the walls, blocks, and pain that have been buried inside that cause you to feel unwhole.

Every spiritual journey is different, just as every Soul is different. At times you will climb the mountains of the Soul and experience the incandescent bliss of Divinity. At other times, you will plunge into the cavernous depths of your inner being and wrestle with long-hidden monsters. However, despite what path you're currently walking, it's vital to remember that any pain or fear you're experiencing is completely normal. All trials and tribulations that you're experiencing right now are working together to fashion you into the awakened being you're destined to become. Like a caterpillar in a cocoon, everything that is not serving your highest good is slowly dissolving away. This discovery, in and of itself, is a huge relief and joyous gift.

By progressing through the three worlds of your spiritual journey (the Upper World, Middle World and Under World), you will be able to meet, discover, and understand any parts of you which have been wounded or repressed. And through Soul Retrieval, you will be able to welcome, release, heal, and integrate these wounded parts through the use of inner child work, self-love, and shadow work. In this book, we've also given you simple exercises and other methods of Soul Retrieval, which you might like to explore further on your journey.

As a part of your spiritual path, it's vital that you're mindful of the traps out there that many people fall into, often for entire lifetimes. We've explored the six most common spiritual bypassing traps earlier in this book. Often these spiritual traps are based on the false beliefs that certain feelings and experiences are "wrong" and therefore should be avoided or denied. The reality is that *all* parts of our nature must be faced and embraced if we are to feel Whole and reconnect with our Souls.

Finally, the culmination of your Inner Work involves learning how to connect with and embody your Soul. When you make a habit of identifying the many signs and omens that appear each day, you will discover that your Soul is always trying to support you in everything you do. Some of the best ways to communicate with your Soul during everyday life include nature immersion, solitude, meditation, connecting with your heart, and prayer. We encourage you to experiment with these ancient healing practices and see how they profoundly impact your life.

The more you consciously commit to retrieving, accessing, and communing with your Soul every day, the more you'll feel grounded, Whole, and at peace. Very soon you'll discover how magical, wise, loving, and supportive life truly is when you're centered in your Soul.

Remember that spiritual awakening is a process. It's an eternal spiral, a dancing mandala, a path with no end. There is no limit to how much you can grow, transform, and embody the Divinity carried within you. The deeper you journey into yourself and the closer you move toward your Soul, the more you rediscover the magic that is always and forever in the present moment. Gradually, you will discover ever-deepening layers of joy, freedom, and peace. Mystics, holy people, and sages throughout the ages have referred to this experience through endless names such as Illumination, Enlightenment, Moksha, Oneness, and Wholeness.

You are now on this sacred path. May you always and forever stay true to your sacred Self.

*"I am not this hair,
I am not this skin,
I am the soul that
 lives within."*

— Jalal ad-Din Rumi

Closing Prayer

Great Spirit who flows through all the Universe, teach me the way.

Teach me to open my heart to forgiveness as I make peace with my past.

Teach me to surrender to the present that I may experience the eternal bliss that is Now.

Teach me to have hope for the future that I may live a life of meaning, purpose, and fulfillment.

As the light of my Soul illuminates my darkness, may I continue to be guided towards truth and liberation.

Although the path is difficult, and the way is steep, I pray that the light of Consciousness brings me home.

Although I will face demons, may the strength of my Soul bring me courage.

Although I will unearth my pain, may the boundless compassion of my True Nature heal all wounds.

Great Spirit, I pray that I may retrieve every lost and disconnected part of my being.

Help me to heal and connect with my inner child.

Support me in my quest to understand and unconditionally embrace my Shadow Self.

As I walk this sacred path, let every barrier obscuring my Everlasting Light dissolve.

As I release every belief, ideal, resentment, and fear that isn't serving my highest good, may I come to embody my Soul.

Thank you for your this spiritual awakening process.

May I come to hear You, see You, feel You, and be with You, each and every day, for You and I are One.

Amen.

References

Alighieri, D. (2016). *The Divine Comedy: The Inferno.* California: Xist Classics.

Avila, T. of, & Cohen, J. (2004). *The Life of St Teresa of Avila by Herself.* London: Penguin.

Bradshaw, J. (1990). *Homecoming: Reclaiming and Championing Your Inner Child.* London: Piatkus.

Brown, J. (2007). *Soulshaping: Adventures in Self-Creation.* Toronto: Pipik Press.

Campbell, J. (2008). *The Hero With a Thousand Faces.* Third Edition. California: New World Library.

Chang, L. (2015). *Americans Spend an Alarming Amount of Time Checking Social Media on Their Phones.* Retrieved August 25, 2016, from http://www.digitaltrends.com/mobile/informate-report-social-media-smartphone-use/

Dossey, L. (1993). *Healing Words.* New York: Harper Collins Publishers.

Estés, Clarissa Pinkola. (2003). *Women Who Run With the Wolves: Myths and Stories of the Wild Woman Archetype.* New York: Ballantine Books.

Fabry, J. B. (1975). *The Pursuit of Meaning.* Dublin: The Mercier Press.

Foster, J. (2016). *The Way of Rest: Finding The Courage to Hold Everything in Love.* Boulder, CO: Sounds True.

Frankl, V. E. (2000). *Man's Search For Meaning: An Introduction to Logotherapy.* New York: Houghton, Mifflin.

Goethe, J. (2014). *Faust: Parts I and II.* London: Nick Hern Books.

Grof, S., & Grof, C. (1989). *Spiritual Emergency: When Personal Transformation Becomes a Crisis.* Los Angeles: Jeremy P. Tarcher.

International Spiritual Emergence Network Directory: http://www.spiritualemergencenetwork.org/find-networks/operating-sens/

James, W. (1994). *The Varieties of Religious Experience.* New York: Random House, Inc.

Johnson, R. A. (2013). *Owning Your Own Shadow: Understanding the Dark Side of the Psyche.* San Francisco: HarperOne.

Jung, C. G. (2012). *Man and His Symbols.* New York: Dell Publishing.

Jung, C. G. (2014). *Modern Man in Search of a Soul.* Oxfordshire: Routledge Classics.

Jung, C. G. (2003). *Psychology of the Unconscious.* New York: Dover Publications.

Lucas, C. G. (2011). *In Case of Spiritual Emergency: Moving Successfully Through Your Awakening.* Forres, Scotland: Findhorn Press.

Maslow, A. H. (1964). *Religious Values and Peak-Experiences.* New York: Penguin Group.

Mistlberger, P. T. (2014). *The Inner Light: Self-Realization Via the Western Esoteric Tradition.* Alresford, Hants: Axis Mundi Books.

Nepo, M. (2011). *The Book of Awakening: Having the Life You Want By Being Present to the Life You Have.* San Francisco: Conari Press.

Nietzsche, F. (2012). *Beyond Good and Evil.* New York: Dover Publications.

ODonohue, J. (2004). *Anam Cara: A Book of Celtic Wisdom.* New York: Harper Perennial.

Price, S., & Haynes, D. (1997). *Dreamworks: A Meeting of Spirituality and Psychology.* Blackburn, Vic: HarperCollinsReligious.

Rea, Rashani. (n.d.) *Poems by Rashani.* Retrieved September 27, 2019, from https://rashani.com/arts/poems/poems-by-rashani

Rūmī, Jalāl-ad-Dīn, & Barks, C. (2010). *The Essential Rumi.* San Francisco: Harper.

St. John of the Cross. (2012). *Dark Night of the Soul.* New York: Dover Publications.

Valiente, D. (1999). *Natural Magic.* London: Robert Hale.

Villoldo, A. (2005). *Mending the Past and Healing the Future with Soul Retrieval.* Carlsbad, CA: Hay House.

Vogler, C. (1999). *The Writer's Journey: Mythic Structure For Storytellers and Screenwriters.* London: Pan.

Walsh, R. N. (2014). *The World of Shamanism: New Views of an Ancient Tradition.* Woodbury, MN: Llewellyn Publications.

Welwood, J. (n.d.) *Human Nature, Buddha Nature: On Spiritual Bypassing, Relationship, and the Dharma – An Interview with John Welwood by Tina Fossella.* Retrieved September 13, 2019, from http://www.johnwelwood.com/articles/TRIC_interview_uncut.doc

Welwood, J. (1995). *Journey of the Heart: Intimate Relationship and the Path of Love.* London: Thorsons.

Bibliography

Cornell, A. W. (1996). *The Power of Focusing: A Practical Guide to Emotional Self-Healing.* Oakland, CA: New Harbinger Publications.

Johnson, R. A. (2009). *Inner Work: Using Dreams and Active Imagination for Personal Growth.* New York: HarperOne.

Jung, C. G., & Shamdasani, S. (2012). *The Red Book: Liber Novus.* New York: W.W. Norton.

Kabat-Zinn, J. (2004). *Wherever You Go, There You Are.* London: Piatkus.

Levine, P. A. (1997). *Waking the Tiger: Healing Trauma.* Berkeley, CA: North Atlantic Books.

Moore, T. (2012). *Dark Nights of the Soul: A Guide to Finding Your Way Through Life's Ordeals.* London: Piatkus Books.

DID YOU LIKE THE SPIRITUAL AWAKENING PROCESS?

Thank you so much for purchasing *The Spiritual Awakening Process*. We're honored that you have chosen our book to help you understand your spiritual journey. We truly hope you've enjoyed this book and now have greater clarity, understanding, and practical advice to apply to your life.

We would like to ask you for a small favor. Would you please take just a minute to leave a review for this book on Amazon or Goodreads? This feedback will help us continue to write the kind of books that will best serve you and others. If you really loved this book, please let us know!

You can also tag us on social media using the hashtag **#spiritualawakeningbook** to let us know your thoughts and feelings about this book!

About the Authors

Aletheia Luna and Mateo Sol are spiritual counselors who united on 11.11.11 and created their popular website *lonerwolf* shortly thereafter. They blend a mixture of psychological and spiritual insight throughout their writings and believe in the value of teaching a down-to-earth approach to spirituality. Their work has been featured and mentioned in respected websites such as The Huffington Post, PsychCentral, and Elephant Journal. To date, they have written over six hundred articles and published numerous books on a variety of spiritual topics.

You can read more of their work and subscribe to their free weekly newsletter on https://lonerwolf.com.

Other Books by the Authors

Twin Flames and Soul Mates

Relationships can be vessels of tremendous mental, emotional, and spiritual growth. In *Twin Flames and Soul Mates,* Luna and Sol teach you how to forge true, deep, and enduring twin flame and soul mate love – no matter what stage you're at, starting right now. Practical, illuminating, and paradigm-shifting, this book is for anyone seeking to find and create an authentic, fulfilling, and conscious relationship in this chaotic world.

Awakened Empath

Written for the highly sensitive and empathic people of life, *Awakened Empath* is a comprehensive map for helping all sensitives everywhere to develop physical, mental, emotional, and spiritual balance on every level. Empaths are people who absorb the emotions of others like a sponge and experiences these emotions as their own. In this book, those who struggle with this unique trait are taught how to strengthen, harmonize, and use their gifts to live life to the fullest and awaken as spiritual beings having a human experience.

Printed in Great Britain
by Amazon